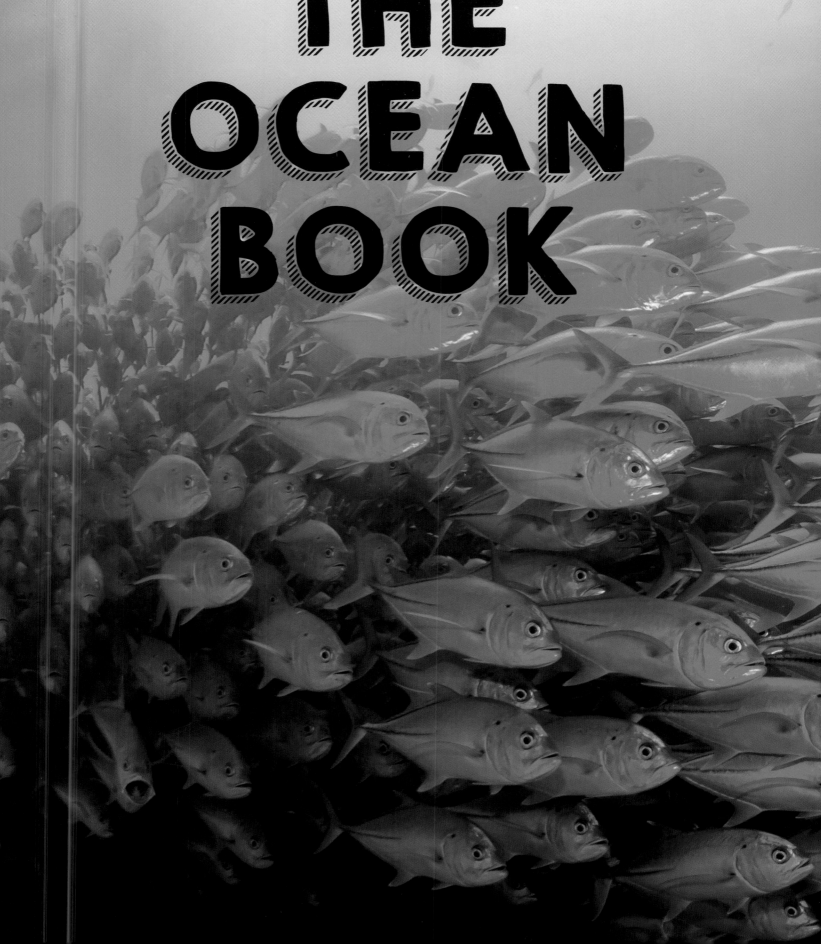

THE
OCEAN
BOOK

ACKNOWLEDGEMENTS

Editorial and Design by Tall Tree Ltd

Author: Derek Harvey
Illustrator: Daniel Limon @ Beehive Illustration
Publishing Director: Piers Pickard
Publisher: Hanna Otero
Art Director: Andy Mansfield
Commissioning Editor: Catharine Robertson
Print Production: Lisa Taylor

With thanks to Jennifer Dixon

Published in September 2020 by Lonely Planet
Global Ltd

CRN: 554153
ISBN: 978 1 78868 237 4
www.lonelyplanetkids.com
© Lonely Planet 2020

Printed in Malaysia
10 9 8 7 6 5 4 3 2 1

STAY IN TOUCH
lonelyplanet.com/contact

Lonely Planet Offices

AUSTRALIA
The Malt Store, Level 3, 551 Swanston St.,
Carlton, Victoria 3053
T: 03 8379 8000

IRELAND
Digital Depot, Roe Lane (off Thomas St.), Digital
Hub, Dublin 8, D08 TCV4

UK
240 Blackfriars Rd., London SE1 8NW
T: 020 3771 5100

USA
Suite 208, 155 Filbert St., Oakland, CA 94607
T: 510 250 6400

THE
OCEAN
BOOK

Explore the hidden depths
of our blue planet

DEREK HARVEY

**CONSULTANT
DR. HELENE BURNINGHAM**

**ILLUSTRATED BY
DANIEL LIMON**

CONTENTS

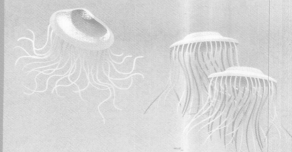

FOREWORD

"It is often said that we know more about the planets of our solar system than we do about the seafloor of the oceans on Earth. What lies beneath the formidable expanse of surface waters can only be seen using specialized equipment. But the oceans play an instrumental role in our lives, driving much of our weather, supporting a significant diversity in animals and plants, and providing us with numerous resources, including food. We have a responsibility to understand and protect our oceans to ensure that they continue to support and provide for all life on Earth in the future."

DR. HELENE BURNINGHAM, COASTAL SCIENTIST

OUR OCEAN PLANET

When viewed from space, our planet looks like a blue marble with swirling white clouds. It might as well be called "Ocean" rather than "Earth" because roughly 70 percent of the surface is salty water. The deepest oceans reach down so far they would cover the highest mountain. And in this vast watery world live some of the most remarkable animals known to humankind.

OCEAN DEPTHS

The average depth of the ocean is about 2.5 mi. (4 km) from the surface to the floor. In some places, huge gashes in the rock go much deeper, reaching down another 3.7 mi. (6 km). Although, compared with the overall diameter of Earth – 7,918 mi. (12,742 km) – these oceans are little more than a thin watery lining on the surface of our rocky planet.

LIVING OCEANS

Our planet might be mostly rock, but it is the surface that matters most to us. This is where we live – together with millions of other kinds of living things. The evolution of life on Earth started in the oceans, and today the water of our rocky planet is teeming with a dazzling array of organisms, from the tiniest floating plankton to the giant blue whale – the biggest animal that has ever lived.

CHANGEABLE OCEANS

A map of the world's oceans might look as familiar to us as a map of our hometown, but the oceans have not always been where they are today. Over billions of years, continents have moved around, broken apart, and collided – driven by forces deep inside the planet. As this happened, oceans have opened wider, shrunk smaller, or disappeared altogether. Today, there are five oceans on planet Earth: Atlantic, Indian, Pacific, Arctic, and Southern.

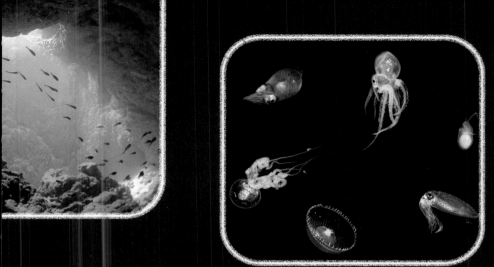

OCEAN HABITATS

As the oceans themselves have changed throughout history, ocean life has changed with them. From the wave-splashed coastlines to the darkest ocean depths, living things have adapted to changing habitats. Huge shoals of fish swim in the nutrient-rich waters around our shores, while some of the strangest animals on the planet live near the ocean bottom.

OCEANS AND HUMANS

We are primates that are adapted to live on land, but that hasn't stopped us from making the most of what the oceans have to offer. We ride on ocean waves to get from place to place, hunt for seafood in ocean waters, and even drill into rocky ocean beds for oil and gas. All around the world, humans swim, dive, sail, and explore.

WHO OWNS THE OCEANS?

Between 1973 and 1982, the United Nations agreed a "Law of the Seas" treaty. This accepts that countries with coastlines own the seas up to 200 nautical miles (a unit that measures distances at sea) out from their land. The rest of the oceans, sometimes called the "high seas," are international waters that are shared by countries for activities such as fishing and navigation.

UNDER THREAT

Sadly, everything we do leaves a mark on our planet. The intensity of our fishing is driving species to extinction, and our garbage and waste have polluted waters. The oceans are even being affected by the way we are changing the planet's climate. But today, more than ever before, people are also recognizing the damage that is being done – and working hard to help protect the oceans and their wildlife.

ATLANTIC OCEAN

The Atlantic Ocean is the second-largest ocean and makes up nearly 30 percent of the world's surface water. Separating the Americas in the west from Europe and Africa in the east, this giant watery world has existed since the time of the dinosaurs! Ancient civilizations sailed on its waves – and more recently, it became the first ocean to be crossed in a boat and a plane.

LABRADOR SEA

HUDSON BAY
Area: 476,000 sq. mi.
(1,233,000 sq km)
Maximum Depth:
850 ft. (259 m)

NORTH AMERICA

CARIBBEAN SEA
Area: 970,000 sq. mi.
(2,512,000 sq km)
Maximum Depth:
25,197 ft. (7,680 m)

MILWAUKEE DEEP

IN A NAME
The name "Atlantic" comes from the Greek god of astronomy and navigation, Atlas. He appeared on many maps from the medieval period, and his name was adopted for modern atlases. The Atlantic separates British and American people and is sometimes referred to as "the pond" – possibly because these nations share many cultural similarities, which makes the ocean between them feel smaller.

GULF OF MEXICO
Area: 596,000 sq. mi.
(1,544,000 sq km)
Maximum Depth:
11,496 ft. (3,504 m)

SOUTH AMERICA

The Greek god Atlas is often pictured carrying the starry sky on his shoulders.

SAILING ACROSS THE ATLANTIC
A Viking called Leif Erikson sailed to North America from Europe in around 1000 CE, 500 years before Christopher Columbus made the same journey in 1492. He is the first known European to have done so.

BALTIC SEA
Area: 148,000 sq. mi.
(382,000 sq km)
Maximum Depth:
1,509 ft. (460 m)

The first transatlantic
flight took 16 hours – and
it was not an easy ride!

NORTH SEA
Area: 222,000 sq. mi.
(575,000 sq km)
Maximum Depth:
2,169 ft. (661 m)

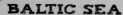

TAKING TO THE SKIES
In 1919, John Alcock and Arthur Brown became
the first people to fly nonstop across the Atlantic.
Using a modified World War I plane, they flew from
Newfoundland in Canada to Ireland.

EUROPE

BLACK SEA
Area: 196,000 sq. mi.
(508,000 sq km)
Maximum Depth:
7,365 ft. (2,245 m)

NORTH
ATLANTIC

MEDITERRANEAN SEA
Area: 969,000 sq. mi.
(2,510,000 sq km)
Maximum Depth:
16,801 ft. (5,121 m)

AFRICA

The ocean is divided
into the North Atlantic
and South Atlantic
by the equator.

**THE ATLANTIC
OCEAN STRETCHES
FROM THE ARCTIC
CIRCLE TO THE
SOUTHERN OCEAN.**

SOUTH
ATLANTIC

Area: 28,771,000 sq. mi. (74,517,000 sq km)
Deepest Point: 28,231 ft. (8,605 m) at
Milwaukee Deep in the Caribbean

ARCTIC OCEAN

At the icy top of the world, the Arctic Ocean is the smallest and shallowest ocean on Earth. With the North Pole at its center, it is almost completely enclosed by the northern coastlines of America and Eurasia. In winter, the ocean is so cold that its surface is almost totally covered in a thick ice sheet, and special icebreaker ships are needed to pass through.

NORTH AMERICA

BEAUFORT SEA
Area: 183,800 sq. mi. (476,000 sq km)
Maximum Depth: 15,364 ft. (4,683 m)

BAFFIN BAY

GREENLAND

WRITTEN IN THE STARS
The name Arctic means "close to the bear" – a reference to the Great Bear and Little Bear star constellations. These patterns of stars are easy to spot in the far northern part of the world and contain the bright North Star.

The Great Bear constellation is also known as Ursa Major.

FINDING THE NORTH POLE
In 1958, the American submarine USS Nautilus became the first submarine to cross the Arctic Ocean beneath the ice sheet. This mission provided proof that the North Pole was underwater, not on land.

USS Nautilus could stay underwater for months – longer than any earlier submarine.

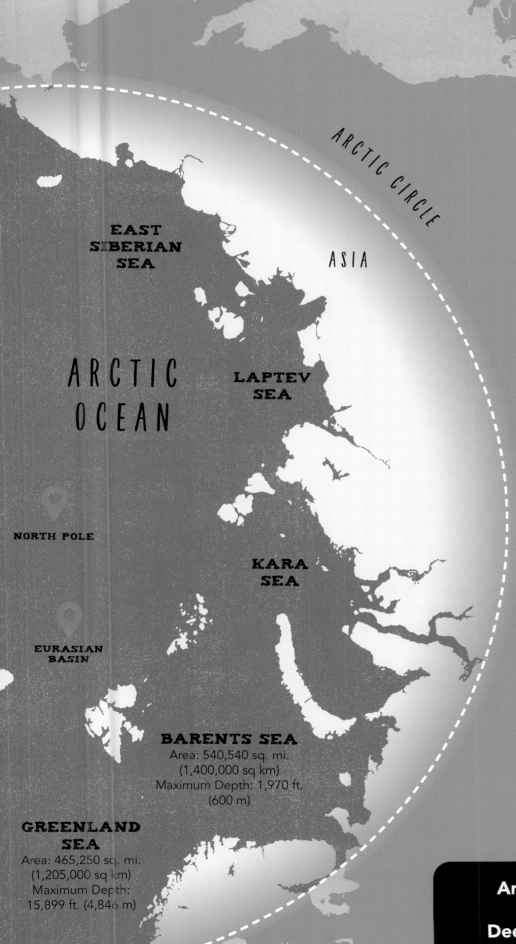

ARCTIC CIRCLE

EAST
SIBERIAN
SEA

ASIA

ARCTIC
OCEAN

LAPTEV
SEA

NORTH POLE

KARA
SEA

EURASIAN
BASIN

BARENTS SEA
Area: 540,540 sq. mi.
(1,400,000 sq km)
Maximum Depth: 1,970 ft.
(600 m)

GREENLAND
SEA
Area: 465,250 sq. mi.
(1,205,000 sq km)
Maximum Depth:
15,899 ft. (4,846 m)

TRICKS OF THE LIGHT

Day and night are unique in the Arctic. In summer, the Sun never fully sets and in winter, it never properly rises. The night skies are often illuminated with the shimmering aurora borealis (northern lights), which look like colorful dancing lights.

The aurora borealis can even be seen by satellites in space!

AS A RESULT OF
GLOBAL WARMING,
THE ARCTIC OCEAN
IS WARMING FASTER
THAN ANY OTHER
OCEAN AND AFFECTING
CLIMATES AROUND
THE WORLD.

Area: 1,965,000 sq. mi.
(5,089,000 sq km)
Deepest Point: 17,880 ft.
(5,450 m) in the Eurasian Basin

INDIAN OCEAN

The third-largest ocean, the Indian Ocean is the only one of the "big three" oceans that doesn't join up with the freezing north. Its warm waters lap the tropical shores around Asia, Africa, and beyond, also affecting the climate of these lands – driving warm weather and seasonal monsoon rains.

EUROPE

PERSIAN GULF
Area: 92,000 sq. mi.
(238,000 sq km)
Maximum Depth:
239 ft. (73 m)

SUEZ CANAL

The Suez Canal is 120 mi. (193 km) long and cuts thousands of miles off many journeys.

RED SEA
Area: 175,000 sq. mi.
(453,000 sq km)
Maximum Depth:
9,974 ft. (3,040 m)

AFRICA

At 3,200 mi. (2,000 km), the Indus River is one of the longest rivers in Asia.

ANCIENT NAME

The name Indian means "from the Indus region" – an ancient area of southern Asia that the country of India is named after. Some of the earliest human civilizations developed in the Indus Valley, and their ocean became an important route for trade between Asia and the rest of the world.

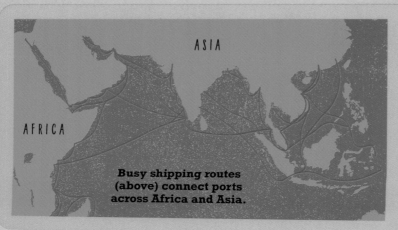

ASIA

AFRICA

Busy shipping routes (above) connect ports across Africa and Asia.

SHIPPING TRAFFIC

This area has many busy shipping routes. It is thought that 40 percent of the world's offshore oil production comes from the Indian Ocean, and huge oil tankers travel across the waters. In 1869, a man-made waterway called the Suez Canal was built to connect the Mediterranean Sea and the Red Sea, providing a shortcut for ships traveling between Europe, North Africa, and Asia, and physically separating the continents of Asia and Africa.

THE SUEZ CANAL

The Suez Canal was originally a much smaller man-made waterway called "The Canal of the Pharaohs," which wound its way through the Egyptian desert. Today, around 50 ships pass down the canal every day, but there isn't enough space for big ships to travel past each other, so they can only travel in one direction!

INDUS RIVER

ASIA

IN 2004, AN EARTHQUAKE OFF THE COAST OF SUMATRA CAUSED A SERIES OF TSUNAMIS THAT HIT COUNTRIES AROUND THE INDIAN OCEAN, WITH WAVES REACHING 66 FT. (20 M) HIGH.

BAY OF BENGAL
Area:
839,000 sq. mi.
(2,172,000 sq km)
Maximum Depth:
14,764 ft.
(4,500 m)

ARABIAN SEA

SUMATRA

JAVA TRENCH

JAVA SEA

INDIAN OCEAN

AUSTRALIA

DRIVING THE WEATHER

A lot of water evaporates from the Indian Ocean because of the warm climate – and that means more rain. Each summer, India and nearby countries, like Vietnam and Thailand, experience a monsoon season of torrential rainfall brought about by a change in wind direction, which sweeps rain inland from over the ocean.

Area: 22,326,000 sq. mi.
(57,824,000 sq km)
Deepest Point: 23,376 ft.
(7,125 m) at Java Trench

13

PACIFIC OCEAN

The Pacific is the largest and deepest ocean of all. Its total area accounts for 46 percent of the Earth's water. When Earth is viewed from space over the Pacific Ocean, it looks practically all blue. The name Pacific means "peaceful" – but around the ocean's outer edge are chains of explosive volcanoes and areas that shake with earthquakes.

SEA OF OKHOTSK
Area: 538,000 sq. mi. (1,392,000 sq km)
Maximum Depth: 11,033 ft. (3,363 m)

BERING SEA
Area: 873,000 sq. mi. (2,261,000 sq km)
Maximum Depth: 13,615 ft. (4,150 m)

ASIA

SEA OF JAPAN
Area: 391,000 sq. mi. (1,013,000 sq km)
Maximum Depth: 12,280 ft. (3,743 m)

PHILIPPINE SEA

CHALLENGER DEEP

MARIANA TRENCH

EAST CHINA SEA
Area: 464,000 sq. mi. (1,202,000 sq km)
Maximum Depth: 8,914 ft. (2,717 m)

THE DEEPEST PART OF ANY OCEAN IS THE MARIANA TRENCH IN THE WESTERN PACIFIC, WHICH PLUNGES DOWN TO 36,000 FT. (11,000 M).

SOUTH CHINA SEA
Area: 1,000,000 sq. mi. (2,590,000 sq km)
Maximum Depth: 18,090 ft. (5,514 m)

CORAL SEA

AUSTRALIA

TASMAN SEA

Ferdinand Magellan made his worldwide voyage in the ship *Victoria* (left).

IN A NAME
In 1521, the Portuguese explorer Ferdinand Magellan was attempting the first voyage around the entire world. After the choppy waters of the southern Atlantic, he rounded the southern point of South America before entering an ocean with calmer winds. He called it *Mar Pacífico* in Latin – meaning "peaceful sea."

Area: 54,486,000 sq. mi. (141,119,000 sq km)
Deepest Point: 36,000 ft. (11,000 m) at Challenger Deep in the Mariana Trench

NORTH
AMERICA

RING OF FIRE

GREAT PACIFIC GARBAGE PATCH

In parts of the ocean, swirling circular currents, called gyres (see page 45), collect floating ocean debris over time – including human trash. The Great Pacific Garbage Patch, in the North Pacific, carries so much plastic that it is estimated to cover an area around three times the size of France.

RING OF FIRE

Around the outer edge of the Pacific, areas of oceanic crust are plunging beneath continents in places called subduction zones (see pages 20–21). No other ocean has quite so many subduction zones. As the rock sinks, it melts and erupts, resulting in chains of volcanoes and earthquakes where the rocky plates shudder and move.

PACIFIC
OCEAN

SOUTH
AMERICA

AN OCEAN OF ISLANDS

There are around 25,000 islands across the Pacific Ocean – more than any other ocean. Most of these are volcanic and many also have additional smaller islands called islets.

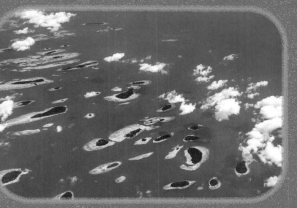

Indonesia has over 17,500 islands and around 6,000 are inhabited.

IF YOU COMBINED ALL THE EARTH'S LAND TOGETHER, ITS TOTAL AREA WOULD BE LESS THAN THE AREA OF THE PACIFIC OCEAN.

SOUTHERN OCEAN

The chilly waters that swirl around the Antarctic continent make up the Southern Ocean. Its waters are teeming with plankton and home to rich marine life, including blue whales – the biggest animal to ever live. Each winter, the Antarctic's ice sheet expands over the ocean surface as temperatures plummet.

GLOBAL REFRIGERATOR

Antarctic currents have an important impact on the other oceans around the world. Cold waters around the outer edge of the Antarctic continent sink and spread outward as they travel northward (see page 45). It is this flow that keeps deep ocean water chilled all over the world – even at the equator.

The Southern Ocean surrounds the frozen continent of Antarctica – home to resilient creatures, like penguins.

THE COLDEST OCEAN WATER ON EARTH IS AROUND THE SHORES OF ANTARCTICA, BUT BECAUSE THE SOUTHERN OCEAN GETS WARMER FURTHER NORTH, OVERALL IT IS NOT AS COLD AS THE ARCTIC OCEAN.

SOUTH SANDWICH TRENCH

WEDDELL SEA
Area: 1,081,100 sq. mi.
(2,800,000 sq km)
Maximum Depth:
9,850 ft. (3,000 m)

RONNE ICE SHELF

BELLINGSHAUSEN SEA

AMUNDSEN SEA

SOUTHERN OCEAN

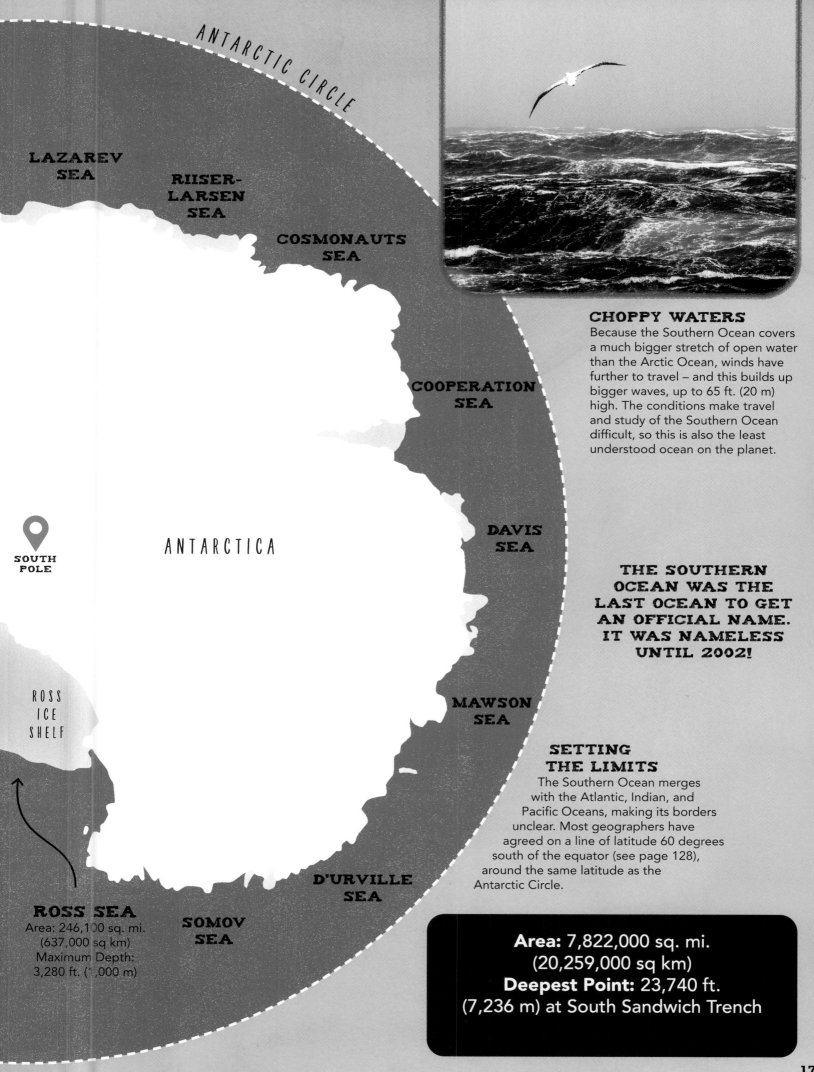

ANTARCTIC CIRCLE

LAZAREV
SEA

RIISER-
LARSEN
SEA

COSMONAUTS
SEA

COOPERATION
SEA

DAVIS
SEA

SOUTH
POLE

ANTARCTICA

ROSS
ICE
SHELF

MAWSON
SEA

D'URVILLE
SEA

ROSS SEA
Area: 246,100 sq. mi.
(637,000 sq km)
Maximum Depth:
3,280 ft. (1,000 m)

SOMOV
SEA

CHOPPY WATERS

Because the Southern Ocean covers a much bigger stretch of open water than the Arctic Ocean, winds have further to travel – and this builds up bigger waves, up to 65 ft. (20 m) high. The conditions make travel and study of the Southern Ocean difficult, so this is also the least understood ocean on the planet.

THE SOUTHERN OCEAN WAS THE LAST OCEAN TO GET AN OFFICIAL NAME. IT WAS NAMELESS UNTIL 2002!

SETTING THE LIMITS

The Southern Ocean merges with the Atlantic, Indian, and Pacific Oceans, making its borders unclear. Most geographers have agreed on a line of latitude 60 degrees south of the equator (see page 128), around the same latitude as the Antarctic Circle.

Area: 7,822,000 sq. mi.
(20,259,000 sq km)
Deepest Point: 23,740 ft.
(7,236 m) at South Sandwich Trench

OCEAN ORIGINS

More than four and a half billion years ago, lumps of rock and ice formed a large disc that swirled around the young Sun. They merged and cooled into rocky planets. On one of the planets, water condensed and rains fell, creating a blue ocean world we call Earth.

Planet Earth

Crust

Inner core

WATER FROM SPACE

Like everything else that makes up our planet, Earth's water originally came from space – either as ice mixed in with the first rocks that crashed together, or in the asteroids and comets that bombarded the Earth after that. But in space terms, there's not much: water accounts for just 0.05 percent of our planet's mass.

OCEANS DEEP – OR OCEANS THIN?

Although Earth's water content seems tiny, it spreads out over more than 70 percent of the surface. The diameter of Earth – from one side to the other through the middle – is 7,926 mi. (12,756 km), but it is just 3.1 mi. (5 km) to the ocean bottom. This means the blueness of our planet is only skin deep, like morning dew that collects on a soccer ball left out on the grass.

TOO HOT FOR OCEANS?

For a long time, scientists thought that for nearly a billion years after it formed, the Earth's surface stayed so hot that any liquid water would have boiled away, leaving a parched, hellish landscape. They called this stretch of time the Hadean Eon, after Hades – the god of the underworld. But then they discovered something that made them change their minds.

ANCIENT CRYSTAL CLUES

When scientists working in Australia analyzed tough little crystals called zircon, they discovered they were formed in the early Hadean Eon. As zircon crystals only form under wet conditions, it showed that our planet had liquid water just 200 million years after it was formed. Perhaps it wasn't so hellish after all.

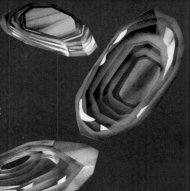

JACK HILLS
AUSTRALIA

Jack Hills in Western Australia contain the minute zircon crystals that were formed in the Hadean Eon and might have been part of an ancient continent called Vaalbara (below). At 4.4 billion years old, they are the oldest materials made on Earth so far discovered.

PACIFIC OCEAN

AUSTRALIA

JACK HILLS

SOUTHERN OCEAN

THE FIRST OCEAN

The young Earth was so hot that its rocks were molten (they had melted) and existed in liquid form. As the Earth cooled about 4.1 billion years ago, it formed a hard crust, and water collecting on its surface became the first ocean. At first, a few erupting island volcanoes would have been the only land. The crust contained a heavy iron-rich rock called basalt that still makes up ocean floors today.

Upper mantle

Lower mantle

Outer core

Continental crust (granite)

Oceanic crust

Heat

Water accounts for just **0.05%** of our planet's mass.

THE FIRST CONTINENT

Heat beneath the surface of the Earth kept deep molten rock moving. Some basalt sank and mixed with light elements, such as aluminum, then floated back to the surface as a rock called granite. After 4 billion years, the lighter rock settled above the oceanic crust (which was heavier) and became the first continent. Fragments of it still exist today in South Africa and Australia.

Vaalbara

A PLANET OF SEA AND LAND

The first continent, named Vaalbara, was much smaller than the continents of today. Back then, the Moon was closer, and its greater gravitational pull would have generated bigger tides lapping Vaalbara's shores. The planet was warm, and its atmosphere was thick with nitrogen and carbon dioxide – and no breathable oxygen. But somewhere in the big ocean, microscopic life was taking hold.

CHANGING OCEANS

The oceans today look permanent, but over millions of years of Earth's history, lands have moved and oceans have come and gone. The Earth's surface crust is in constant motion – in some parts of the world it plunges into trenches, or new molten rock bubbles up from the deep.

BROKEN CRUST

Around 4 billion years ago, the Earth emerged from its violent formation in the Hadean Eon into the milder Archean Eon. During this time – but we're not sure why – its crust shattered into fragments called tectonic plates, and these began to move around due to the currents of molten rock that churned underneath. Some plates were under ocean, others were under continents, and some spread across the two.

MOVING PLATES

Tectonic plates move very slowly, about as fast as a human fingernail grows, but over millions of years, this can shift entire continents and oceans. The biggest effects are where neighboring plates meet. Here, plates ram into one another, move apart, or slide past one another, causing earthquakes and volcanoes. This is also where oceans or continents can be made or lost.

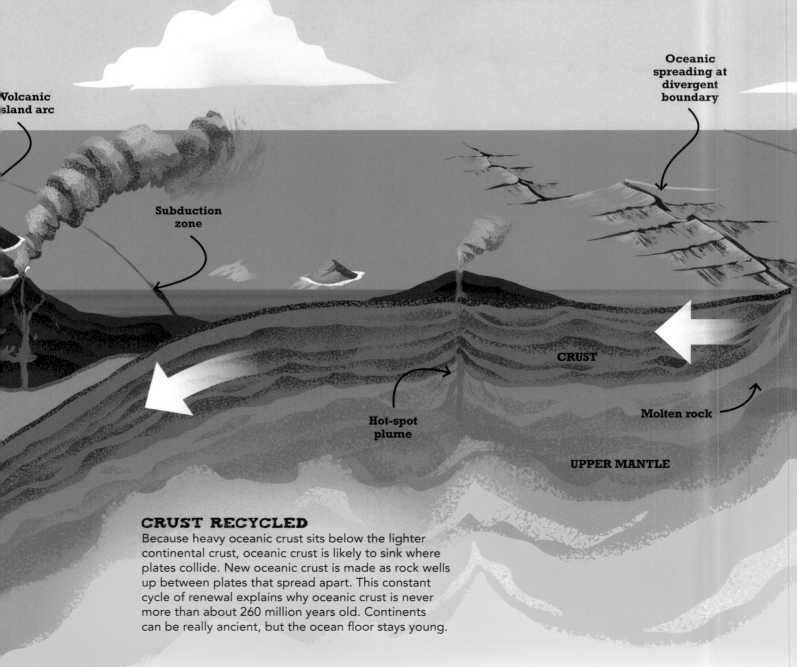

Volcanic island arc

Subduction zone

Oceanic spreading at divergent boundary

Hot-spot plume

CRUST

Molten rock

UPPER MANTLE

CRUST RECYCLED

Because heavy oceanic crust sits below the lighter continental crust, oceanic crust is likely to sink where plates collide. New oceanic crust is made as rock wells up between plates that spread apart. This constant cycle of renewal explains why oceanic crust is never more than about 260 million years old. Continents can be really ancient, but the ocean floor stays young.

NEW OCEAN FLOOR

As plates move apart, molten rock erupts below and builds up on either side of the gap. This is called a divergent boundary because the plates are moving in different directions (diverging), and it is happening down the middle of the Atlantic Ocean today. Here, new ocean floor is constantly being created along a volcanic ridge that runs from north to south – pushing America and Africa further apart.

Divers exploring the Mid-Atlantic Ridge.

Subduction zone

Oceanic crust

Continental crust

SUBDUCTING PLATE

DISAPPEARING OCEAN FLOOR

Plates moving toward one another meet (converge) at a convergent boundary. If this happens on land, lighter continental crust can buckle up into mountain ranges. When an oceanic plate meets a continental plate, the heavier oceanic crust dives down under the other – a process called subduction. Where two oceanic plates collide, the heaviest one will plunge into an ocean trench and sink into the mantle.

EURASIA

NORTH AMERICA

AFRICA

SOUTH AMERICA

INDIA

AUSTRALIA

ANTARCTICA

PANGAEA

HOW OCEANS DISAPPEAR

Sometimes, tectonic plates drive continents closer together. If oceanic crust gets pulled into a trench at a convergent boundary and is not replaced at a divergent boundary, the gap between continents closes. This has happened many times in Earth's history, as continents have merged into "supercontinents" and the oceans between them have disappeared. The most recent example is Pangaea, which formed around 300 million years ago.

JAVA TRENCH
INDIAN OCEAN

The Java Trench to the west of Sumatra is the deepest part of the Indian Ocean and is formed where the Indo-Australian Plate under the Indian Ocean plunges beneath the Eurasian Plate under Indonesia. As the plate sinks, heat and pressure build, causing a chain of active volcanoes to rise up through the islands of Indonesia.

MALAYSIA

INDONESIA

JAVA TRENCH

INDIAN OCEAN

THE FIRST LIFE

Evidence suggests that the first life on Earth may have begun more than 4 billion years ago – just a few million years after the planet was formed. For more than 3 billion years, living things stayed microscopic and single-celled, but their presence had a big impact on the world at the time.

LIFE FROM NON-LIFE

No one knows for sure how the first living thing developed from the nonliving materials in the young Earth, but scientists have developed ideas based on studies of organisms alive today. Most think this happened in the oceans, where rich mixtures of chemicals became the building blocks for life.

LIFE'S CRADLE

Many scientists think life began in the deep ocean around volcanic vents where water is warm. These underwater "chimneys" still throw out rich mixtures of chemicals today. Over 4 billion years ago, the chemical-rich waters might have reacted with minerals in rocks, kick-starting a chemical reaction that helped bring the materials for life together and forming the first microscopic single cells.

Volcanic vents look like underwater chimneys spewing clouds of chemicals.

EARLY LIFE DIVERSIFIES

The Archean Eon lasted from 4 billion to 2.5 billion years ago. This was when continents grew and microscopic life multiplied into lots of different forms. The first organisms probably harnessed energy from the chemical reactions happening in their underwater home. Even today, some bacteria use chemical energy in the same way (see page 53). Meanwhile, other prehistoric microbes evolved different ways to survive, by preying on other microbes around them.

Stromatolites are rock-like formations that can provide evidence of Earth's earliest microbes.

OCEAN LIFE BECOMES SOLAR-POWERED

At the end of the Archean Eon, microbes spread into shallower sunlit water from the deep ocean floor and found a new source of energy: sunlight. They used light to generate energy-rich food from carbon dioxide and hydrogen, which they got from the water around them. This process is called photosynthesis, and they became the first living things to do this – with momentous consequences.

SHARK BAY
AUSTRALIA

Stromatolites are mounds of tightly packed sediment left behind by some of the first communities of photosynthesizing microbes, more than a billion years ago. Living stromatolites are still forming today and can be seen scattered in coastal seas of the world, including Shark Bay.

PACIFIC OCEAN

AUSTRALIA

SHARK BAY

SOUTHERN OCEAN

AN OXYGEN CRISIS

When hydrogen is split away from water, it leaves oxygen – so photosynthesizers (living things that photosynthesize) released oxygen into the atmosphere. Until then, the Earth's oxygen had been bound to other elements and locked in the rocks, so single-celled life was not used to it. Oxygen killed off most early life, whereas today, most life needs oxygen to survive.

Algae contain chlorophyll for photosynthesis.

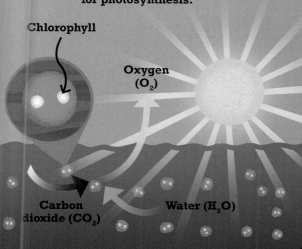

Chlorophyll

Oxygen (O_2)

Carbon dioxide (CO_2)

Water (H_2O)

SNOWBALL EARTH

Photosynthesizers in the ocean also sucked carbon dioxide out of the atmosphere to make their food – and this affected the world's climate. Carbon dioxide helps to trap in heat and without it, the Earth's temperature dropped. For a while, our planet turned into a freezing ball covered in snow and ice.

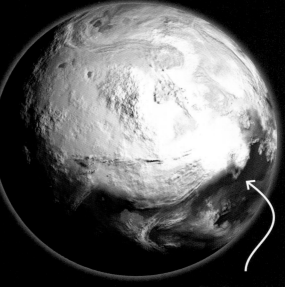

Earth may have been nearly entirely frozen 2.25 billion years ago!

LIFE ADAPTS

But life has a way of dealing with a crisis: it evolves new ways of coping. Some organisms survived snowball Earth and adapted to turn oxygen to their advantage. They used it to extract more energy from food – just as burning fuel generates heat. This made them so efficient that oxygen kick-started a spurt in evolution that ended up filling the oceans with life.

LIFE FILLS THE OCEANS

Life became a runaway success as conditions in the oceans encouraged living things to evolve into many more different kinds. For the first time, life became bigger and more complex. Single-celled microbes formed bigger bodies of algae and, eventually, animals made up of billions or trillions of working cells.

SUPEROCEAN

The ancient Vaalbara continent (see page 19) broke apart 2.5 billion years ago when the Archean Eon gave way to the Proterozoic Eon (meaning "early life"). New crust formed, creating the seeds of modern continents, including North America, Africa, and Australia. But these lands were in very different positions from where they are today. Around a billion years ago, they had joined into another single giant continent called Rodinia, surrounded by a superocean called Mirovia.

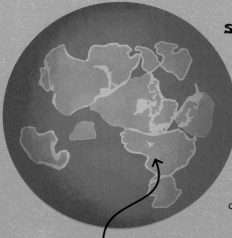

Rodinia
supercontinent

FROZEN SEAS

Rocks dating from the time of Mirovia show that 700 million years ago, the Earth froze (again). Scientists think that carbon dioxide in the atmosphere, from volcanic eruptions, might have been flushed out of the air by heavy storms. This fall in carbon dioxide, a greenhouse gas that traps heat, made temperatures plummet, creating one of Earth's biggest ice ages. Mirovia might have frozen to a depth of 1.2 mi. (2 km)!

Marks on "trace fossils" show animal activity.

Weird soft-bodied creatures glided along the ocean bottom.

THE FIRST MOVING ANIMALS

Despite the extreme conditions, life survived once again. Tracks and impressions in fossils from around 600 million years ago show that animals had evolved muscles for moving about – some of them were evidently crawling and burrowing on the ocean bottom.

PIONEERS ON THE OCEAN FLOOR

The first ocean-floor animals probably lived by grazing on carpets of microbes or algae. Fossils also show that other animals sprouted tall leaf-like stalks that waved about in the currents, most likely absorbing drifting food particles. Many of these pioneers were unlike any animals alive today.

This strange, symmetrical organism may have been one of Earth's earliest animals.

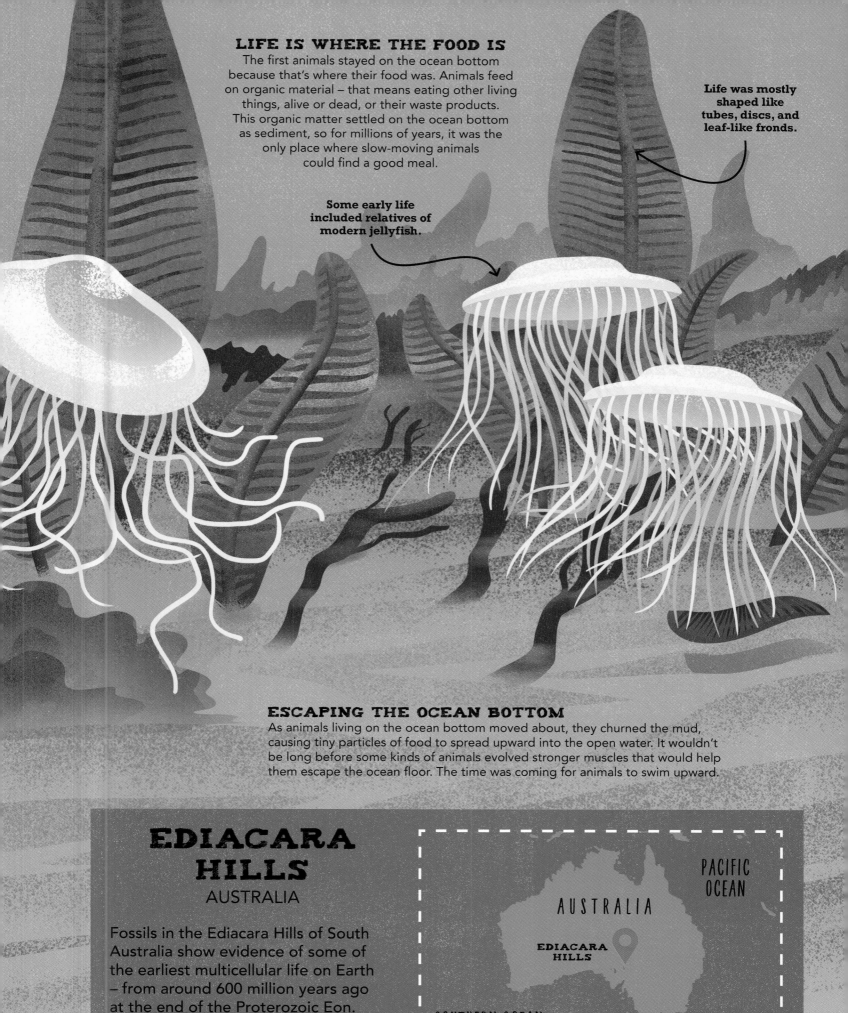

LIFE IS WHERE THE FOOD IS

The first animals stayed on the ocean bottom because that's where their food was. Animals feed on organic material – that means eating other living things, alive or dead, or their waste products. This organic matter settled on the ocean bottom as sediment, so for millions of years, it was the only place where slow-moving animals could find a good meal.

Life was mostly shaped like tubes, discs, and leaf-like fronds.

Some early life included relatives of modern jellyfish.

ESCAPING THE OCEAN BOTTOM

As animals living on the ocean bottom moved about, they churned the mud, causing tiny particles of food to spread upward into the open water. It wouldn't be long before some kinds of animals evolved stronger muscles that would help them escape the ocean floor. The time was coming for animals to swim upward.

EDIACARA HILLS
AUSTRALIA

Fossils in the Ediacara Hills of South Australia show evidence of some of the earliest multicellular life on Earth – from around 600 million years ago at the end of the Proterozoic Eon.

PACIFIC OCEAN

AUSTRALIA

EDIACARA HILLS

SOUTHERN OCEAN

RISE OF COMPLEX OCEAN LIFE

The Paleozoic Era started about 540 million years ago and was a time when animal life exploded in diversity in a way never seen before. This was when corals, snails, fish, and many other recognizable kinds of animals first appeared.

The start of the Paleozoic Era was called the Cambrian Period. Evolution of animal life at this time is often likened to an explosion because it has left so many more fossils than the periods before. This rise might be due to the fact that many animals were forming hard shells, called exoskeletons, that left better traces when fossilized than earlier soft-bodied animals.

OPEN-WATER SWIMMERS
The first fish-like animals that swam in open water had a flexible rod called a notochord, which supported their backs. As they moved forward, water streamed into their mouths and out through slits in the sides of their heads, where gills extracted oxygen to help them breathe. Fossils from 525 million years ago show that early fish had eyes, and a brain enclosed in a rubbery casing called cartilage.

Haikouichthys was one of the earliest known fish.

Pirania was a type of sea sponge (now extinct).

Opabinia had a segmented body and fan-shaped tail.

ARMORED FISH
During the Silurian Period (part of the Paleozoic Era) about 440 million years ago, fish had bodies supported by a more solid material: bone. It replaced the flexible notochord to make a spine. The first big group of fish, called ostracoderms, evolved bony armor to protect their bodies. But these fish had one big disadvantage: they didn't have jaws, so couldn't bite.

Ostracoderms had protective body armor.

BITING FISH
Because ostracoderms couldn't bite, they relied on sucking small, slow prey into their mouths. When a new group of fish, called placoderms, evolved bony hinged jaws, they became much more formidable. The biggest, called *Dunkleosteus*, lived around 370 million years ago. It grew to around a ton in weight and became the first giant predator of the oceans.

Dunkleosteus was large and fierce.

CHANGING CONDITIONS
Even placoderms didn't last – they became extinct around 100 million years after they first appeared. No one is quite sure what caused this, but around this time, the oceans were changing. Plants started to colonize the land and nutrients from soil flushed into the sea from rivers, perhaps causing microbes to thrive and use up all the oxygen.

Vast swamp forests dominated land in the Carboniferous Period.

THE CAMBRIAN OCEAN

At the start of the Cambrian Period, the ancient supercontinent had changed shape and began to break up, forming a new ocean, the Iapetus Ocean, between the pieces. This helped to drive evolution of even more animal types, as smaller landmasses meant longer shorelines for organisms that thrived in sunlit shallow waters.

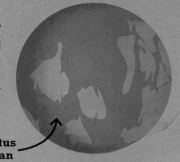

Iapetus Ocean

Shrimp-like *Anomalocaris* was a top predator.

Trilobites could curl into balls, like woodlice.

***Hallucigenia* was a spiky worm-like animal.**

BURGESS SHALE
CANADIAN ROCKIES

One of the best fossil beds from the Cambrian Explosion is the Burgess Shale, in the Canadian Rockies, which dated at 508 million years old. It contains evidence of an extraordinary diversity of ancient soft-bodied invertebrate animals, mostly living on the seafloor. They are preserved in prehistoric mud from just before the first appearance of fish.

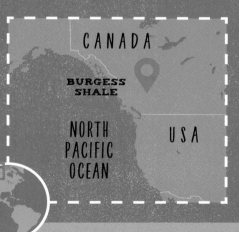

CANADA

BURGESS SHALE

NORTH PACIFIC OCEAN

USA

***Cladoselache* grew up to 6 ft. (1.8 m) long.**

ANCIENT SHARKS

Other ocean animals filled the place of predatory placoderms: sharks. The first sharks lived alongside the placoderms but had a different body design. Their skeletons were made from cartilage rather than bone, which made them more lightweight. Sharks still exist today (of course) — they are some of the biggest fish in our modern oceans and among the largest underwater predators.

BONY FISH

Today, more than 95 percent of fish have a skeleton made from bone. This makes them heavier than sharks, but most fish have a gas-filled swim bladder, which makes them buoyant in water. Bony fish diversified into practically every ocean habitat and even started venturing into freshwater rivers and lakes.

AGE OF THE REPTILES

By 250 million years ago, backboned life had colonized the land: fleshy-finned fish had evolved into amphibians and reptiles with legs. But as their descendants gave rise to dinosaurs, some returned to water and became giant reptiles of the sea.

LIFE BETWEEN LAND AND SEA

When four-legged fish – the first amphibians – crawled out of water more than 350 million years ago, much of the land was covered with warm, wet swamp forest. A hundred million years later, the land was joined together into a C-shaped supercontinent called Pangaea, enclosing the Paleo-Tethys Ocean. The Panthalassic Ocean covered the rest of the globe.

Panthalassic Ocean

PANGAEA

Paleo-Tethys Ocean

PARCHED LAND

The age of the reptiles started about 250 million years ago. The climate was hot and dry due to volcanic eruptions flooding the atmosphere with carbon dioxide, trapping heat. But scaly-skinned reptiles were perfectly adapted. Their evolution over the next 2 million years gave rise to groups that would include the dinosaurs, some of the biggest land animals ever to have existed.

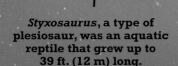

Styxosaurus, a type of plesiosaur, was an aquatic reptile that grew up to 39 ft. (12 m) long.

ICHTHYOSAURS

While dinosaurs rose to rule the lands, other groups of reptiles returned to the oceans. Among them were ichthyosaurs. These dolphin-like predators may have been warm-blooded, unlike cold-blooded reptiles. This meant that they could maintain a steady body temperature. Ichthyosaurs escaped the need to lay eggs on land by giving birth to live young in the water, just like dolphins and other fully aquatic mammals do today.

Ichthyosaur may have looked similar to a porpoise.

PLESIOSAURS

More giant ocean reptiles followed the ichthyosaurs, which failed to adapt to changing climates fast enough. Some plesiosaurs evolved very long necks and were among the biggest marine predators of the time. They also gave birth to live young, and as ichthyosaurs began to die out, the plesiosaurs multiplied.

OCEANS AT THE TIME OF GIANT REPTILES

When dinosaurs walked the land and plesiosaurs swam in the ocean, the continents had split into two chunks: Gondwana in the south and Laurentia in the north. Between the two was the wide Tethys Ocean. At the height of the giant reptiles, Gondwana began to fragment again, eventually becoming South America, Africa, India, Australia, and Antarctica.

The two supercontinents gradually broke into modern-day continents.

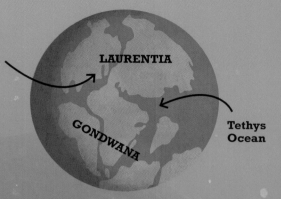

LAURENTIA

GONDWANA

Tethys Ocean

Some giant mosasaurs grew up to 56 ft. (17 m) long!

OCEAN REPTILES AT THEIR PEAK

Other groups of reptiles evolved in the oceans at the time of the dinosaurs, including mosasaurs. These were distant cousins of snakes, but swam with flippers, just like the ichthyosaurs and plesiosaurs. Giant reptiles shared the oceans with sharks and other prehistoric fish, but their time would not last.

MASS EXTINCTION

Earth's history has suffered several catastrophic events that wiped out much of life each time in mass extinctions. The most famous happened around 66 million years ago, when an asteroid or comet collided with the Earth, throwing gas and dust into the atmosphere, and blocking out the Sun's energy. All the giant reptiles, including ichthyosaurs, plesiosaurs, and mosasaurs, as well as dinosaurs on land, were lost.

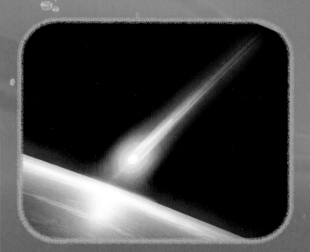

JURASSIC COAST
ENGLAND, UK

The "Jurassic Coast" is a stretch of rocks that runs along the southwest coast of England. The rocks date back to the time of the dinosaurs, and a huge number of fossils have been found here, including those of the prehistoric ocean reptiles ichthyosaurs and plesiosaurs.

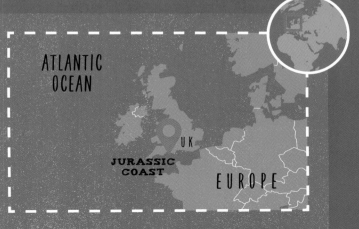

ATLANTIC OCEAN

UK

JURASSIC COAST

EUROPE

AGE OF THE MAMMALS

In the wake of the mass extinction that killed the giant reptiles, a new group of backboned animals succeeded them: mammals. These had stayed small and shrew-like during the time of the dinosaurs, but when the giants disappeared, mammals started changing into many different forms. Those evolving in the oceans became the dolphins and whales that are alive today.

NEW OCEANS

When dinosaurs became extinct, the continents were splitting from north to south, opening into what would become the Atlantic Ocean. At this time, mammals on land were growing bigger – becoming the ancestors of familiar modern-day animal groups, such as hoofed mammals and meat-eating carnivores.

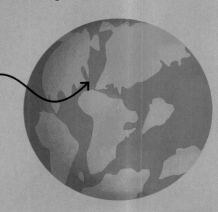

The Americas in the west and Europe-Africa in the east were pushed further apart.

Pakicetus walked on land but is thought to be a distant cousin of whales.

WHALE ANCESTORS

By 50 million years ago, the shapes of the continents were beginning to look similar to those of today. Their positions had opened up into the modern oceans: Atlantic, Indian, and Pacific. Somewhere along the southern Asian coastline, a strange amphibious mammal – a cousin of modern hippopotamuses – was the distant ancestor of whales and dolphins. Called *Pakicetus*, it looked a bit like an upright crocodile with fur.

MAMMALS INVADE THE OCEANS

Pakicetus (left) was only 3 ft. (1 m) long and had walking legs, but probably ventured into freshwater, too. In the same part of the world, a larger relative called *Ambulocetus* later spent time between the land and the sea. It had evolved paddle-shaped feet and a strong tail that flapped up and down to propel it underwater.

THE FIRST WHALES

Ambulocetus did not spend all its time in the water, but by around 40 million years ago, other mammals did. *Basilosaurus* looked much more like a true whale. Its front feet were flippers, and its hind feet were tiny. It had a flat horizontal tail called a fluke, much like a whale's, and nostrils higher on its head so it could come to the surface to breathe.

The tail of a *Basilosaurus* looked similar to a modern-day whale's tail.

CHANGING DIET

The land-living ancestors of whales were hippo-like herbivores. In the oceans, they needed a new way of feeding. *Ambulocetus* had strong teeth for catching fish. Later forms, such as *Aetiocetus*, combined teeth with brush-like plates called baleen that strained water for food. Eventually, modern baleen whales lost their teeth altogether and relied entirely on filtering small planktonic organisms, such as krill.

Megalodon: 59 ft. (18 m)

Great white shark: 20 ft. (6 m)

WHY DID WHALES EVOLVE SO BIG?

The bigger the whale, the more food it could strain! By 20 million years ago, their huge baleen-filled mouths could filter thousands of krill with every mouthful of seawater. Predators may also have driven whales to become giants – in particular, a giant shark called *Megalodon*. It was three times bigger than its modern relative, the great white shark, and probably preyed on whales at the time. We know this from bite marks in their fossilized bones!

WADI EL HITAN
EGYPT

Wadi El Hitan in Egypt is a World Heritage Site that preserves ocean life from around 40 million years ago. Since the first discoveries in 1902, many ancient whale fossils have been found – including the fossilized skeleton of a *Basilosaurus*.

MEDITERRANEAN SEA

WADI EL HITAN

LIBYA

EGYPT

SUDAN

OCEAN WATER

Ocean water contains a similar amount of salt all around the world. But other conditions change from place to place; the warm sunlit shallows at the tropical equator are very different from the cold polar regions.

Ocean water is **96.5%** water

\+

3.5% salts and other substances, of which...

55% Chloride

31% Sodium

14% Other (magnesium, sulfur, calcium, and potassium)

SEAWATER SALT

On average, ocean water contains about 5 oz of salt to every gallon of water. Most of this salinity is due to sodium chloride – common salt – the same stuff that you might have on your kitchen table. Sea salt also contains other chemicals, and many of these extra chemicals are used by ocean organisms to stay alive.

DILUTIONS AND CONCENTRATIONS

Freshwater from melting ice, rain, and rivers dilutes the ocean's salt. Big rivers, such as the Amazon, send so much freshwater into the ocean that the dilution affects the water far out at sea. In contrast, in some enclosed seas or bays, the water is warm enough to turn into water vapor – a process called evaporation. The salt is left behind, so evaporation makes the water saltier.

Salt increases the density of the water, so saltier seas are easier to float in.

WHY IS SEAWATER SALTY?

The first oceans, formed 4.4 billion years ago, were made from fresh rainwater that pooled over the Earth's crust. Over time, salts from the rocks and soil were swept away by river water and built up in the ocean. Salt levels have stayed about the same for billions of years – and most ocean life has been forever adapted to the concentrations found in seawater today.

Evaporation of seawater

Precipitation of rain or snow

Freezing of seawater

Melting of ice

River runoff

INCREASED SALINITY (MORE SALTY)

DECREASED SALINITY (LESS SALTY)

Groundwater flow to ocean

TEMPERATURE

Oceans are notably warmer in the tropics than they are at the poles, particularly around the coast, where seas are shallower. Compared with land, underwater temperatures do not vary as much as temperatures of the air. This is because water needs to gain or lose a lot more heat to significantly change temperature.

Surface temperatures range from 28°F (-2°C) in the Arctic Ocean to 81°F (27°C) in the Indian Ocean.

Microscopic algae called phytoplankton produce oxygen.

LIGHT

Light travels through the ocean because water is transparent. But there are limits to how far down light can reach. Sunlight is a mixture of all the colors in the rainbow, and each color has a different wavelength. All wavelengths ultimately get absorbed by water, but blue wavelengths can travel much deeper. Some blue light is reflected back to our eyes, making the ocean look blue.

OXYGEN

Most life needs oxygen to survive. Oxygen makes up 21 percent of the air we breathe. As ocean waves churn, they mix oxygen from the air into the water. Cold water holds more oxygen than warm water because gases are more likely to escape at warmer temperatures. There is also more oxygen near the surface. This is because the algae living there produce oxygen through photosynthesis.

RED SEA
INLET OF THE INDIAN OCEAN

Like some other enclosed seas, the salt concentration of the Red Sea, at an average of 6 oz per gallon, is higher than that of the ocean. Few freshwater rivers run into it, and high levels of evaporation under the heat of the surrounding deserts makes it extra salty. It's easier to float in the Red Sea because the salt helps to hold you up!

LIBYA
EGYPT
RED SEA
SAUDI ARABIA
IRAN
SUDAN
ERITREA
YEMEN
OMAN
INDIAN OCEAN

OCEANS AND THE WATER CYCLE

Since the Earth was formed 4.5 billion years ago, the amount of water it contains has stayed about the same. All water on Earth is recycled, moving between the liquid in oceans, gaseous vapor in the air, and solid ice. As water evaporates from Earth's surface and then falls as rain or snow, it drives the water cycle.

WHERE IS THE WATER?

Unsurprisingly, the oceans make up the biggest fraction of water on Earth. They contain nearly 97 percent of the water on our planet! The remaining water is divided between ice and land – including freshwater lakes and rivers, and water held in the ground (together just over 3 percent). A final tiny fraction is up in the atmosphere as gaseous vapor, which can form clouds.

0.1%

The smallest fraction of water is in the atmosphere, where it can form clouds.

97%

Almost all of the world's water is held in the oceans.

3%

A small portion of water is held in polar ice caps...

...and in lakes, rivers, and water in the ground.

DRIVING THE CYCLE

As energy from the Sun warms the top layers of the ocean, some of this energy is transferred to tiny water molecules. By having more energy, molecules can escape from the surface into the air. On average, about 459 million cubic feet of water evaporate from the oceans every second (just 6 cubic feet equal about 1 bath full!). But this is still a tiny fraction of the total amount of water held in all the oceans.

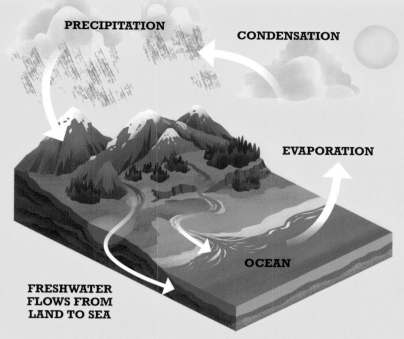

PRECIPITATION

CONDENSATION

EVAPORATION

OCEAN

FRESHWATER FLOWS FROM LAND TO SEA

WATER IN THE ATMOSPHERE

Water escaping from the ocean due to evaporation becomes water vapor and mixes with other gases that make up the Earth's atmosphere. As the vapor rises, it gets cooler and the water eventually condenses (turning from a gas into a liquid) back into droplets that make up clouds.

FALLING RAIN

As water droplets get bigger, they reach a point where they are too heavy to stay floating inside the clouds. When this happens, they fall as precipitation – either as rain, snow, or hail, depending on how cold it is. More clouds form over the oceans than land because more evaporation has taken place there. Overall, precipitation over the ocean roughly balances evaporation from it, and water levels stay about the same.

THE IMPORTANCE OF THE OCEAN IN THE WATER CYCLE

Because of the huge volume and surface area of the oceans, they account for about 85 percent of the Earth's global water evaporation, and 77 percent of all precipitation falls on the ocean surface. But ultimately, even water falling over land eventually enters the oceans through rivers and streams. Around 330 million gallons of river water empties into the oceans every second!

DRAKE PASSAGE
WHERE THE ATLANTIC MEETS THE PACIFIC

In some parts of the world, like in the 497 mi. (800 km) wide Drake Passage between South America and Antarctica, heavy rainfall combined with strong winds can result in ocean storms that are among the most ferocious on the planet. Sailing here can be treacherous and boats have to be equipped to battle the elements, including violent thunderstorms and giant waves.

PACIFIC OCEAN

SOUTH AMERICA

ATLANTIC OCEAN

DRAKE PASSAGE

SOUTHERN OCEAN

ANTARCTICA

OCEANS AND THE CARBON CYCLE

The chemical element carbon exists in all living things and makes up many complex substances in our bodies. It is constantly being recycled through living and nonliving things: plants and animals, the atmosphere (as carbon dioxide), the ocean, soil and sediment, and in chalky rocks.

A WORLD WITH CARBON

Carbon is a key ingredient in the complex substances found in living bodies – such as carbohydrates, protein, and DNA. Outside these bodies, it also exists as the gas carbon dioxide in the atmosphere, and in chalky carbonate in rocks.

Chalk is a form of limestone that contains carbon.

CARBON DIOXIDE IN WATER

Carbon gets recycled because chemical reactions change it from one form to another – and the oceans play a big part in this. Carbon dioxide in the atmosphere is chemically changed by rainwater or ocean water, forming a weak acid, some of which turns into a substance called hydrogen carbonate. Today, increased carbon dioxide from polluted air is making the oceans more acidic, which is harming marine life.

SHELLS FROM WATER

Dissolved hydrogen carbonate can react to form a solid chemical called calcium carbonate. Many living things in the ocean use this to build their shells. They include rocky corals as well as microscopic organisms of the plankton family, called foraminifera.

ROCK FROM SHELLS

Foraminifera have lived in oceans for millions of years. When they die, their tiny shells sink to the bottom and build up on the ocean floor in their trillions to form layers of sediment. Eventually, this sediment gets compacted and cements together to form a chalky rock called limestone.

Foraminifera have tiny protective shells.

MOUNT EVEREST
HIMALAYAN MOUNTAINS

Can you believe that the tallest mountain on Earth used to be underwater? Mount Everest may seem a long way from the sea but it is topped with limestone. This rock formed on the seabed of a prehistoric ocean that was thrust upward when India collided with Asia 50 million years ago!

CHINA

MOUNT EVEREST

NEPAL

INDIA

Limestone is formed from the fossilized shells of sea creatures over millions of years.

CARBON IN THE FOOD CHAIN

The recycling of carbon through rock accounts for about 660 million tons of carbon each year. But even this is just a tiny fraction of the carbon passing through the global carbon cycle. Living things – not just shelly ones – have 10 times more impact on the carbon cycle due to carbon recycled in their bodies via food chains (see pages 42–43).

Shells contain calcium carbonate that marine animals extract from water.

CARBON DIOXIDE FROM FIRE

The carbon inside chalky rock gets returned to the atmosphere in a dramatic way. When volcanoes erupt, they spew out hot molten rock. The heated carbonates in the rock break down to release carbon dioxide back into the air – so the carbon cycle can begin again.

THE OCEAN SEASCAPE

Ocean basins are like huge bowls carved out of the Earth's crust, inside which the oceans sit. They are bordered by shallow seas that lap the coasts of continents. Further offshore, the seabed plunges steeply down until it reaches the ocean bottom. The dark ocean depths are the least explored and least understood parts of the Earth's surface.

Continental shelf

North Pole

Siberian Shelf

Asia

The Siberian Shelf is the largest in the world.

CONTINENTAL SHELVES

Each continent is surrounded by a rim of land that is submerged by shallow ocean waters. This is the continental shelf, where water is typically no deeper than 492 ft. (150 m). Most continental shelves stretch no more than 50 mi. (80 km) out to sea, but they can be wider. The Siberian Shelf stretches 932 mi. (1,500 km) northward into the Arctic Ocean!

Shallow coastal seas sit above continental shelves.

Continental shelf

Continental slope

Continental rise meets the abyssal plain.

CONTINENTAL SLOPES AND RISES

Beyond the edge of a continental shelf, the seafloor slopes gently downward – turning into a continental slope. As it gets deeper, the slope starts to flatten, turning into the continental rise. When the seabed reaches the very bottom of the ocean, it is then called the abyssal plain.

ABYSSAL PLAIN

More than 50 percent of the Earth's surface is made up of the flat ocean floor. This is the abyssal plain, and it can vary from 1.8–3.7 mi. (3–6 km) deep. The seabed here is largely smooth because there is nothing down here like weather to disturb it. But in some places across the abyssal plain, volcanic rumblings from deep inside Earth, and erupting vents, disturb the peace.

VENTS AND SEEPS

Hydrothermal vents (see pages 110–111) are cracks in the oceanic crust of the abyssal plain through which heated seawater and molten rock erupts. These usually occur along the borders of tectonic plates. Elsewhere, cold seeps can be found, where gases including methane and hydrogen sulfide gas, as well as salt, seep up out of the seafloor. These often form weird underwater brine pools that collect on the ocean bed.

RISING SEAMOUNTS

Underwater mountains, called seamounts, are scattered across parts of the abyssal plain – sometimes rising up to 2.5 mi. (4 km) from the ocean floor. These are left by underwater volcanoes, often long extinct. Many do not reach the surface, but the tips of some form islands, such as the Hawaiian Archipelago in the Pacific.

DEEP, DARK TRENCHES

As the tectonic plates that make up the Earth's crust slowly move, some plate edges on the abyssal plain get pulled down into the Earth, carving deep underwater trenches. The Mariana Trench, in the Eastern Pacific, is the deepest in the world, reaching down to nearly 6.8 mi. (11 km). These are the deepest and most mysterious parts of the ocean.

Continental rise

Seamounts rise up from the seabed, forming islands.

Oceanic trenches are deep chasms in the abyssal plain.

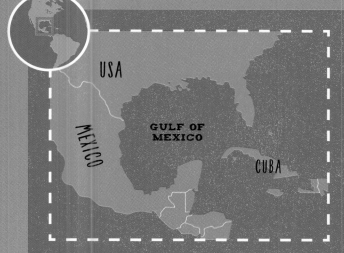

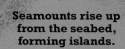

USA

MEXICO

GULF OF MEXICO

CUBA

GULF OF MEXICO
ATLANTIC OCEAN

Despite their name, cold seeps on the ocean floor are actually warmer than the surrounding ocean water (but cooler than hydrothermal vents!). The most active cold seep area is under the Gulf of Mexico – where "pools" of brine on the ocean bottom are four times saltier than normal seawater. Seep mussels and tube worms live here, using chemicals within the pool to generate energy (see page 111).

CONDITIONS AT DEPTH

One of the biggest factors that affects living conditions for ocean life is depth. The habitat on the deepest ocean floor can be as different from conditions at the surface as a forest is from a desert. Deeper water changes in many ways: it gets colder, darker, and the pressure increases.

SUNLIGHT TO MIDNIGHT ZONES

The surface is the brightest zone, called the sunlight zone. Down to a depth of 656 ft. (200 m), waters are rich with algae and the animals that eat them. Below this, down to 3,280 ft. (1,000 m), is the dimly lit twilight zone, and deeper still is the midnight zone – where all is pitch black. Not only are deeper zones colder and at higher pressure, they have less food, too.

SUNLIGHT ZONE

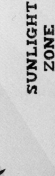

Tuna

Dolphin

Jellyfish

TEMPERATURE

Water at the surface of the ocean, down to about 656 ft. (200 m) in depth, is warmer at the tropical equator than at the cold poles – and all over the world the temperature drops with depth. The biggest drop happens several hundred feet below the surface at a point called the thermocline. From here, temperatures slide down gradually toward the ocean bottom, where they hover just above freezing.

LIGHT

Below 656 ft. (200 m), the water is dim because very little light can travel this far, and below 3,280 ft. (1,000 m), no light reaches at all. Life here lives in perpetual darkness, with no obvious change from day to night. Any light at these depths comes from special light-producing chemical reactions in the bodies of certain animals. This process is called bioluminescence.

TWILIGHT ZONE

Octopus

Swordfish

Catshark

OXYGEN

At the surface, oxygen is added to the water by photosynthesizing algae and churning waves, but below the surface, levels of oxygen drop. The lowest levels are several hundred feet down, where oxygen-using microbes feast on particles of food that sink down from above. Below this, oxygen levels slowly rise again as there are fewer living things to use it up.

Hatchetfish

Squid

SEA LEVEL

656 FT. (200 M)

3,280 FT. (1,000 M)

Sperm whale

MIDNIGHT ZONE

Sea cucumber

Anglerfish

Bristlemouth fish

Starfish

Rattail fish

PRESSURE

Pressure increases with depth and is measured in atmospheres. One atmosphere is the pressure experienced at sea level. Below the surface, one additional atmosphere is added for every 33 ft. (10 m) of depth. So at 16,000 ft. (5,000 m), near the ocean bottom in many parts of the world, it is 500 atmospheres – more than enough to crush a car!

ZONATION AT DEPTHS

Temperature, oxygen levels, and pressure change the environment in a big way, and creatures at different depths have adapted to live with these changes. This variation in communities of species as the depth increases is called zonation. Most kinds of animals stick to one particular zone, but some migrate up and down and pass between zones.

ABYSSAL ZONE

Tube worms

HADAL ZONE

CHALLENGER DEEP
PACIFIC OCEAN

The deepest part of the ocean is a section of the Mariana Trench called Challenger Deep. It is named after the ship HMS *Challenger* that first measured its depths in 1875. Challenger Deep plunges down to 35,853 ft. (10,928 m). If you submerged Mount Everest here, there would still be over 6,600 ft. (2,000 m) of water above its peak!

MARIANA TRENCH

PHILIPPINES

PACIFIC OCEAN

13,123 FT. (4,000 M)

19,685 FT. (6,000 M)

36,089 FT. (11,000 M)

OCEAN FOOD CHAIN

Food chains in the ocean channel energy from sunlight through living things. They begin when algae on the surface photosynthesize, using sunlight to make food and oxygen. The algae are then eaten by animals, which are eaten by bigger predators in turn. At each link in the food chain, the energy in food gets passed from one organism to another.

STARTING AT THE SURFACE

Algae are part of a group of tiny organisms called phytoplankton. These phytoplankton are eaten by microscopic drifting animals, such as shrimps and fish larvae, called zooplankton. The chain continues, passing energy from creature to creature, as smaller ocean animals are eaten by bigger predators.

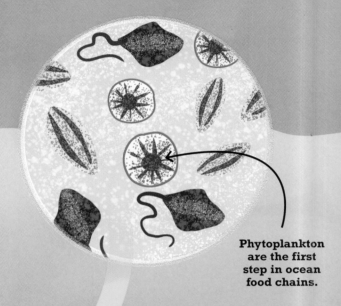

Phytoplankton are the first step in ocean food chains.

OCEAN FOOD-MAKERS

Algae are organisms that can photosynthesize, like plants do on land. They use energy from sunlight to make sugar from carbon dioxide and water. Many algae are microscopic single cells, and trillions of them live close to the ocean surface. Here, they suck huge amounts of carbon dioxide out of the atmosphere to make their food.

Microscopic creatures called zooplankton feed on phytoplankton.

Small fish feed on the zooplankton.

OCEAN DECOMPOSERS

In the oceans, nothing gets wasted – dead material gets broken down by decomposers, including bacteria and other microbes. This process starts in the open water and finishes when dead particles have sunk to the ocean bottom. Here, scavenging animals, such as hagfish (left) and some sharks, vacuum up anything that's left.

A whale carcass provides a feast on the seafloor.

WHERE THE ENERGY GOES

At each level in a food chain, some energy is lost as waste and heat, so less is available to be passed on. This means that there are fewer bigger predators compared with the trillions of tiny plankton at the beginning of the food chain. Ultimately, just a tiny fraction of the energy from sunlight striking the ocean surface ends up in bodies of big predators at the top of the food chain.

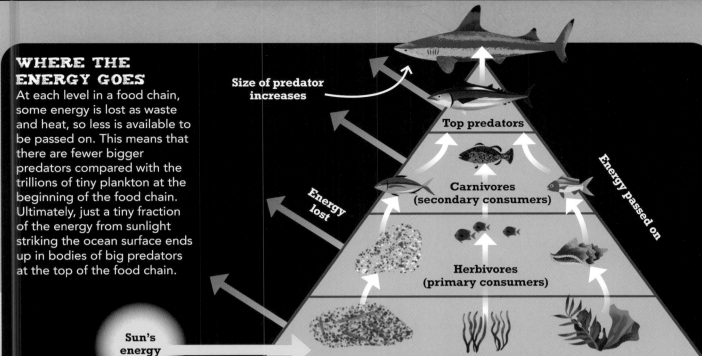

Size of predator increases

Top predators

Energy passed on

Energy lost

Carnivores (secondary consumers)

Herbivores (primary consumers)

Sun's energy

Plants (producers)

Smaller fish are eaten by bigger fish, and the energy is passed on.

TOP OCEAN PREDATORS

Eventually, the energy that was gathered by photosynthesizing algae ends up in the flesh of the biggest ocean predators, such as great white sharks, orcas, and sperm whales. Many of these animals are very big, but because there are fewer of them, their total combined weight is less than the combined weight of all the smaller animals further down the food chain.

Particles of waste matter sink down from above as "marine snow."

CARBON DOWN - AND UP

The deep ocean is too dark for photosynthesizing algae, but animals still live there. They survive by eating food that sinks down from above – either dead or dying creatures and phytoplankton, or particles of organic matter, including waste from other animals. When living things breathe, carbon is released as carbon dioxide. This goes back into the surroundings and eventually returns to the air where it begins the cycle again.

LIFE WITHOUT LIGHT

Most animals living on the ocean floor still rely on the Sun because they depend on food chains that began at the surface. But in some places on the seafloor, microbes get their energy out of volcanic minerals that are spewed out of hydrothermal vents (see page 111). These microbes form the basis of deep-sea food chains that exist entirely independent of the Sun.

OCEAN CURRENTS

The waters of the ocean are constantly moving. Currents swirl around the globe, moving water between the surface and the deep. These currents mix up ocean water, scattering nutrients and warmth, helping to prevent the climate on land from getting too extreme.

WIND-DRIVEN CURRENTS

Winds push the surface layers of the ocean, affecting water down to about 164 ft. (50 m) deep. Sunshine warms the air, making it expand and reducing its pressure; wind then blows, as air flows from a higher to a lower pressure.

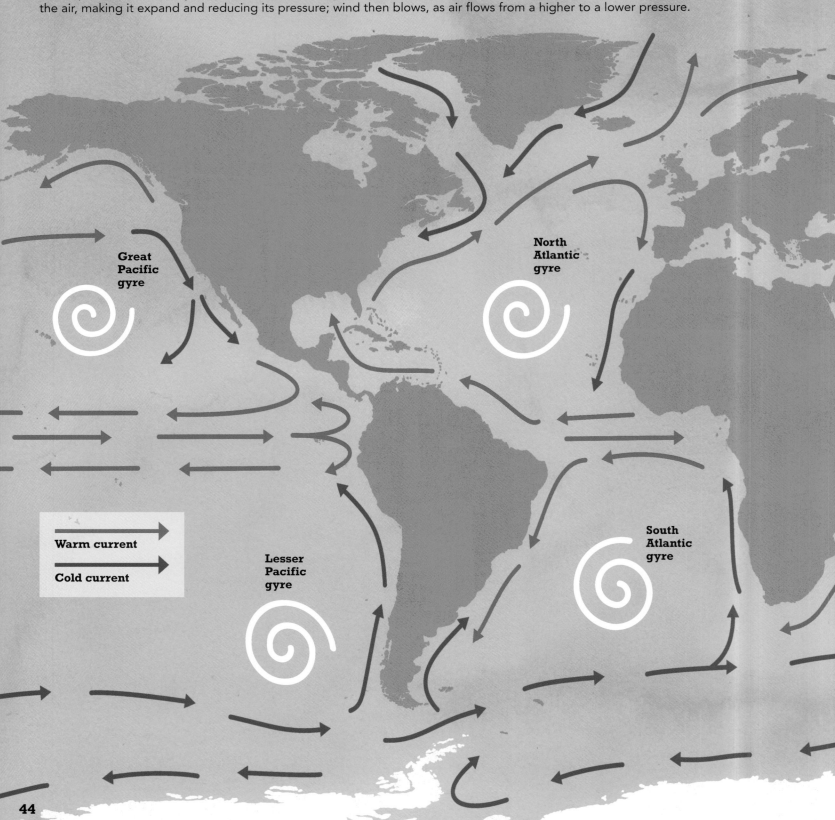

Great
Pacific
gyre

North
Atlantic
gyre

Warm current

Cold current

Lesser
Pacific
gyre

South
Atlantic
gyre

CIRCUMPOLAR CURRENTS

Westerlies are winds that flow from west to east around the globe in both hemispheres, between the equator and the poles. In the southern hemisphere, the oceans are uninterrupted around Antarctica, so westerlies here make ocean currents circulate. This creates the Antarctic Circumpolar Current, which is the world's largest ocean current, pushing water right down to the seabed.

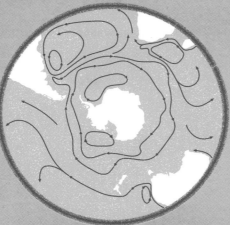

TEMPERATURE AND SALT

As well as wind, water currents are caused by differences in temperature and salt concentration, called salinity (see pages 32–33). As warm ocean water flows from the tropics to the poles, it cools down and loses its energy, getting denser and saltier as the molecules move closer together. Eventually, the cool water sinks, helping to mix surface waters into the deep.

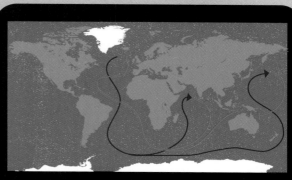

THERMOHALINE CIRCULATION

These temperature and salinity effects generate a global flow of water called the thermohaline circulation ("thermo" meaning "temperature," "haline" meaning "salinity"). Warm surface waters sink in the North Atlantic, then flow slowly southward, eventually rising back to the surface in other places, such as the North Pacific. It can take 1,000 years for deep ocean water to reach the surface in this way.

GYRES

Air flowing from the cold poles to the warm equator gets knocked off course because of the spinning of the Earth – this is called the Coriolis effect. This process helps to set up circular patterns of currents in the oceans, called gyres. In the northern hemisphere, they rotate in a clockwise direction; in the southern hemisphere, they rotate counterclockwise.

Clockwise

Counterclockwise

UPWELLINGS

Winds that flow along coastlines can get diverted out to sea by the Coriolis effect (see Gyres, above). This pushes surface water away from land and deeper water rises up to replace it. It brings nutrients from near the seabed closer to the surface, nourishing growing algae and enriching food chains along the coast. This water from the deep is called an upwelling.

Indian Ocean gyre

Wind blowing along coastline

Water moving out to sea

Upwelling   45

WAVES AND TSUNAMIS

Even the calmest ocean is covered with ripples, as tiny waves pass across its surface. Those small waves can grow very big, rising feet above the surface and crashing onto coastlines with extreme force.

Wind blows across the surface.

ENERGY OF WAVES

Although waves that break on the shoreline look like they are moving water from the ocean to the land, this is not the case. In fact, the water molecules within a wave are moving in a circular motion and only the water's energy moves across the surface; the water itself doesn't move much at all. This is why a floating seabird bobs up and down as a wave passes, but only moves forward if there is a current.

Wavelength

WAVE CREST

WAVE CREST

Circular movement of water molecules

WAVE TROUGH

HOW WIND CREATES WAVES

Most waves are caused by wind blowing across the ocean surface and pushing the water up into a wave crest. Stronger winds that blow for a longer time generate bigger waves. Waves also grow bigger when they travel across wider expanses of water, a distance called the fetch. This is why bigger waves form over the open ocean than across lakes with a smaller surface area.

WAVE SHAPES

The peaks (highest points) of waves are called crests, while the dips (lowest points) between waves are called troughs. Crests can vary in height, and the distance from one crest to another, called the wavelength, varies, too. Big waves with higher crests are more likely to do damage when they crash onto the shore because they carry more energy than smaller waves.

WAVE BEHAVIOR

A breaking wave sweeps water called swash up the shore, before it runs back into the ocean in the backwash.

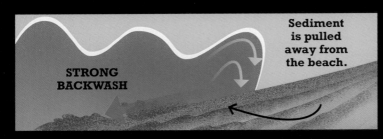

Sediment is pulled away from the beach.

STRONG BACKWASH

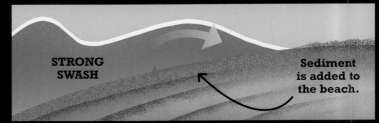

STRONG SWASH

Sediment is added to the beach.

Waves with higher, more frequent crests tend to create stronger backwash. This causes sediment to be removed from the beach, wearing it away.

Smaller, less frequent breaking waves tend to add sediment (such as rock particles from the sea) to the beach because the swash is usually stronger than the backwash.

NAZARÉ
PORTUGAL

The wind-driven Atlantic waves that break on the Portuguese coastline are thought to be among the largest in the world. In 2017, surfer Rodrigo Koxa set the world record for the highest wave surfed at Nazaré. It was 79 ft. (24 m) high from trough to crest!

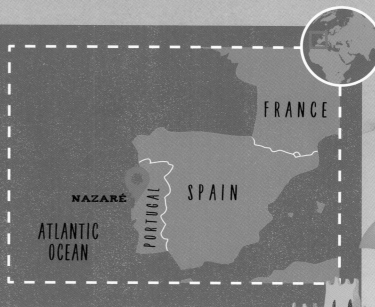

FRANCE

NAZARÉ

PORTUGAL

SPAIN

ATLANTIC OCEAN

Breaking wave gains height

BREAKING WAVES

Waves that start out in the open ocean eventually hit obstacles or coastlines. Shallower coastal water interrupts the base of the wave, slowing it down. Because the crest keeps moving forward faster than the base, the wave breaks, toppling over and crashing onto the shore.

THE EFFECT OF COASTLINES

Coastlines that are exposed to wider expanses of open ocean water are more likely to be battered by big waves that have built up across a long fetch. Other coastlines that are in sheltered bays experience less wave action because the waves are interrupted by other land before they enter the bay, which reduces their energy.

A sheltered bay generally has smaller waves.

In 2011, waves around 128 ft. (39 m) tall hit the coast of Japan after an earthquake at sea.

TSUNAMIS

The biggest waves of all are generated not by surface winds but by disturbances deep below the ocean surface. Underwater earthquakes, landslides, or volcanic eruptions can push against the water to create a wave with a very long wavelength. This means that it hits the shore with a very high crest and can travel far inland as a tsunami, causing devastating damage.

TIDES

The actions of tides are among the most predictable aspects of ocean behavior. Just as night follows day, the tides typically sweep up and down our shorelines twice in every 24-hour period. And what makes this happen is something far beyond our planet.

WHAT ARE TIDES?

Tides are the rise and fall of sea levels that happen because of the gravitational pull of the Sun and the Moon, as well as the rotation of the Earth. The pull makes Earth's water periodically bulge outward, making sea levels higher. In fact, a tide is really a giant, very slow-moving wave moving across the globe.

A WORD ABOUT GRAVITY

Objects the size of planets, moons, and stars are so big that their gravity pulls on other objects around them – and the bigger and closer the object, the bigger the pull. Our Moon's gravitational pull is experienced on Earth as the ocean's tides.

EFFECT OF THE MOON

As the Earth spins, different parts of its surface face the Moon, which pulls the ocean toward it to create the bulge of high tide. The opposite side of the Earth, furthest from the Moon, also has a high tide because the pull is weakest here, so the ocean bulges away from the Moon. This means that for any point on Earth, a bulge happens twice for every complete spin, explaining why tides occur twice within 24 hours.

Low tide

High tide

SUN

Gravitational pull of Sun

MOON

Gravitational pull of Moon

EARTH

Low tide

Moon's orbit

EFFECT OF THE SUN: SPRING TIDES

The Sun is further away than the Moon but it is so much bigger that its gravitational force is also felt. When the Sun and Moon line up, which happens twice a month at the full Moon and new Moon, the tides are bigger than usual. These are called spring tides (though they have nothing to do with the season).

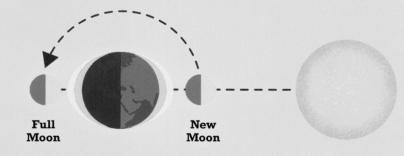

Full Moon

New Moon

SPRING TIDE

NEAP TIDES

The Sun has a smaller effect as it moves further out of line with the Moon. This means its smallest influence happens when it is at right angle to the Moon. These smaller tides are called neap tides. Again, they happen twice a month, but this time at first quarter and third quarter moons.

TIDES ALONG COASTS

Tides are not noticeable in the middle of the ocean, where there is no point of reference. It is along the coastlines that we see them, as ocean water rises up to flood the land or ebbs away to expose it. The time between one high (or low) tide and the next is usually just under 12.5 hours, so there are two high tides and two low tides within a 24-hour day.

High tide

Low tide

LOCAL EFFECTS

Tides are also affected by the shapes of coastlines and the underwater seabed because these landforms alter the flow of water. In some parts of the world, the tidal pattern is changed so much due to the position of the land that there is only a single high tide each day. And when an incoming tidal flow is channeled through a narrow bay or river, it can create an impressive fast-moving wave called a tidal bore.

High tide

NEAP TIDE

First quarter Moon

Third quarter Moon

SOUTH KOREA

JAPAN

CHINA

QUIANTANG RIVER

EAST CHINA SEA

QIANTANG RIVER
CHINA

The world's largest tidal bore happens in the mouth of the Qiantang River in China, where the tide can produce a wave of water up to 30 ft. (9 m) high, traveling at 25 mph (40 kph). People visit to watch or surf the giant wave, which is locally dubbed the "Silver Dragon."

WHERE IS THE OCEAN LIFE?

Living things find a way of surviving everywhere in the ocean, from the wave-splashed edges, where the water meets the coast, right down to the deep ocean bottom. Life is richest where there is light or food, but every part of the ocean has its own set of organisms adapted to the conditions around it.

Seagulls nest in coastal cliffs and feed on seafood.

Sea turtles lay their eggs on land and feed at sea.

VISITORS FROM LAND AND AIR
Some animals spend most of their time on land and only visit the ocean to feed. These animals, including seabirds and seals, are all air-breathers and give birth to their young on land. Other air-breathing animals, such as turtles, spend virtually all their life in water, but come ashore briefly to breed.

Portuguese man-of-war jellyfish float at the surface.

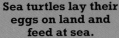

Gannets are birds that dive from a height of 98 ft. (30 m) to catch fish!

FLOATERS
A few ocean organisms spend most of their lives floating on or near the surface of the water. They include the Portuguese man-of-war, a relative of the jellyfish, and sargassum – a kind of seaweed. Both have air-filled chambers, called bladders, that keep them afloat. The Portuguese man-of-war gets its name from its air-filled bladder, which looks like the sail of an old Portuguese warship.

OPEN-WATER DRIFTERS
Many organisms don't control their movements and simply drift in the ocean. Some can swim but are too weak to fight the flow and so they move with the currents. These drifters are part of the ocean's plankton. Most planktonic organisms are tiny or even microscopic – such as single-celled algae, or the larvae of fish and crabs. But some larger weak-swimming fish, like the ocean sunfish, are types of plankton, too.

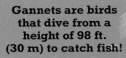

This giant sunfish is one of the largest fish in the ocean, but its weak swimming ability makes it part of the plankton.

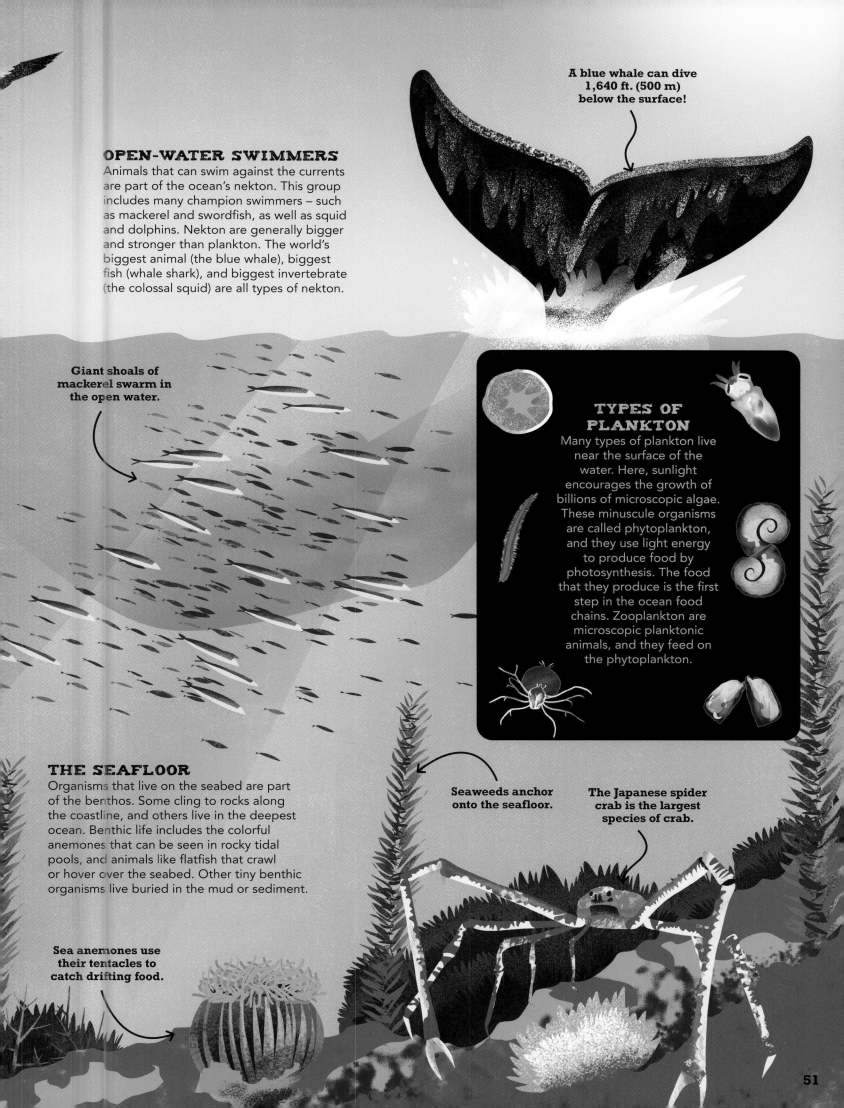

OPEN-WATER SWIMMERS

Animals that can swim against the currents are part of the ocean's nekton. This group includes many champion swimmers – such as mackerel and swordfish, as well as squid and dolphins. Nekton are generally bigger and stronger than plankton. The world's biggest animal (the blue whale), biggest fish (whale shark), and biggest invertebrate (the colossal squid) are all types of nekton.

A blue whale can dive 1,640 ft. (500 m) below the surface!

Giant shoals of mackerel swarm in the open water.

TYPES OF PLANKTON

Many types of plankton live near the surface of the water. Here, sunlight encourages the growth of billions of microscopic algae. These minuscule organisms are called phytoplankton, and they use light energy to produce food by photosynthesis. The food that they produce is the first step in the ocean food chains. Zooplankton are microscopic planktonic animals, and they feed on the phytoplankton.

THE SEAFLOOR

Organisms that live on the seabed are part of the benthos. Some cling to rocks along the coastline, and others live in the deepest ocean. Benthic life includes the colorful anemones that can be seen in rocky tidal pools, and animals like flatfish that crawl or hover over the seabed. Other tiny benthic organisms live buried in the mud or sediment.

Seaweeds anchor onto the seafloor.

The Japanese spider crab is the largest species of crab.

Sea anemones use their tentacles to catch drifting food.

MICROBES AND ALGAE

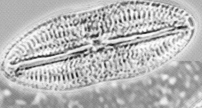

Even the tiniest living things can be some of the most important. Ocean water is teeming with single-celled organisms that are so small you need a microscope to see them. Near the sunlit surface, microbes make food just like plants on land. Deeper down, other microbes help recycle waste matter. These tiny living things are vital to life on Earth.

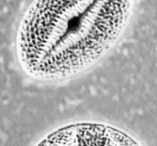

SOLAR-POWERED MICROBES

If you scoop up a cupful of ocean water, it might contain hundreds of thousands of little green cells: these are the photosynthesizing algae, or phytoplankton. They come in all shapes and sizes, and produce at least 50 percent of the oxygen made on Earth! There are diatoms with sculptured shells, dinoflagellates that swim by beating microscopic whip-like threads, and cyanobacteria – the tiniest solar-powered organisms of all.

Some flakes of marine snow fall for weeks before reaching the ocean floor.

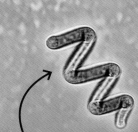

MICROSCOPIC SCAVENGERS

Just like on land, the oceans are full of natural recyclers that eat dead and waste material. The biggest of these are animals, such as worms, and the tiniest are microbes, such as bacteria. Microscopic bits of debris floating in the water stick together to form bigger visible particles called "marine snow." These sink and settle on the bottom, where bacteria feed on them.

Some cyanobacteria are spiral shaped.

Diatoms have silica shells that are like thin glass cases.

Over 1,500 species of dinoflagellates exist in the oceans.

MAINE
USA

Sometimes, environmental conditions, like temperature, nutrient level, and wind direction, cause an overgrowth of coastal algae called a "bloom." In places such as Maine in the US, there can be so much red-colored algae that the water looks red! You wouldn't want to swim here; the algae contains toxic chemicals that can kill fish and make shellfish dangerous to eat.

CANADA

MAINE

USA

ATLANTIC OCEAN

THE SMALLEST PREDATORS

The tiniest algae and bacteria are preyed on by another set of microbes that are just a bit bigger, but still too small to see with the naked eye. These single-celled predators, called ciliates, propel themselves forward by beating hairs and swallow live prey into their miniature gullets (throats).

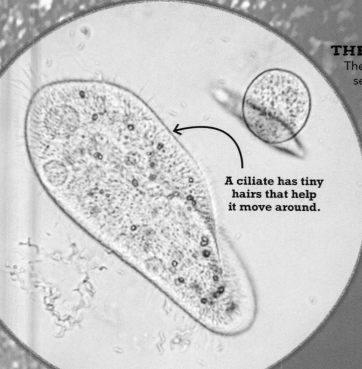

A ciliate has tiny hairs that help it move around.

MICROBE MATS

Many microbes, including cyanobacteria and diatoms, release a kind of slime that helps them stick to sediment, stopping them from being washed away by currents. Sediment and microbes build up in layers, called mats, on the muddy seafloor around coastlines.

STROMATOLITES

In certain places around the world, mats made of cyanobacteria build up with layers of sediment to form rocky mounds called stromatolites. These mounds provide records of ancient life on Earth, with fossils that formed 3.7 billion years ago! Today, other hungry organisms usually eat them before they grow, except in lagoons that are too salty for grazing animals.

Living stromatolites in sunlit waters can be thousands of years old.

MAKING FOOD IN DARKNESS

Bacteria living around volcanic vents on the ocean floor are some of the strangest microbes of all. Like algae at the surface, they make food, but they do so without light energy from the Sun. Instead, they are powered by the energy that is released by chemical reactions around the vents. This kick-starts the only known food chains on Earth that exist without the Sun.

SEAWEEDS AND TRUE PLANTS

From ancient forests to city streets, plant life can grow almost anywhere on land. But hardly any true plants can grow in the oceans because the conditions are so different – and those that do are restricted to muddy coastlines. Everywhere else, the ocean's vegetation is dominated by big leafy algae called seaweed.

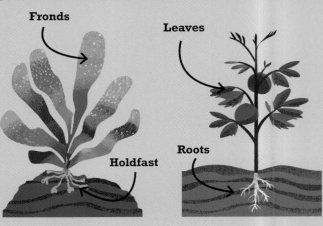

Fronds

Leaves

Holdfast

Roots

SEAWEED

PLANT

WHAT ARE SEAWEEDS?

Seaweeds don't grow in the same way as true plants, even though they have leaf-like parts, called fronds, that can photosynthesize. Instead of roots, seaweeds usually have a sucker-like base, called a holdfast, that attaches to coastal rocks. A few kinds float freely in the ocean.

TYPES OF SEAWEEDS

All seaweeds are a type of big plant-like algae, called macroalgae. Brown seaweeds are some of the most familiar kinds found on seashores, where thick patches are exposed at low tide. They are only distantly related to plants. Red seaweeds, found in deep water, and green seaweeds are both closer cousins of true plants.

These bubbles of air are called "air bladders."

BROWN SEAWEEDS

There are different types of brown seaweeds, including wracks and kelps. The clumps of seaweed that you see exposed at low tide are usually wracks. Some wracks have air bladders that are like tiny air-filled balloons. These help their fronds float at high tide, so they can gather more light energy. Kelps have long, strap-like fronds and can form huge underwater kelp "forests."

RED AND GREEN SEAWEEDS

Red and green seaweeds survive less well in air and prefer to grow in places that are usually underwater, although some also live in rock pools. Stringy green seaweed called gutweed grows especially well in places where it is fed by nutrients from freshwater that runs off the land.

WHY THE DIFFERENT COLORS?

All seaweeds contain green chlorophyll to help them absorb sunlight. Other color pigments, like red and brown, might act like a kind of sunscreen. Seaweed that is exposed to direct sunlight at low tide often looks more brown in color as these pigments help protect it from the Sun's fiercest rays.

Seagrasses have roots and leaves and produce seeds, like plants on land.

WHERE ARE THE PLANTS?

Why do so few true plants grow in the ocean, where seaweeds grow so well? For a start, roots cannot take hold on bare rock. Also, most plants cannot tolerate salt because it draws water from their cells, making them dehydrated. Only a few kinds of plants manage to survive on coastal mud.

Mangroves are plants that have adapted to live in salty water, with wide roots to support them on mud.

SEAGRASSES, SALT MARSHES, AND MANGROVES

Seagrasses are just about the best ocean-adapted true plants of all. In many parts of the world, they form extensive underwater meadows that are completely submerged. Nearer to dry land, other salt-tolerant plants form salt marshes (see pages 92–93). And in the tropics, salt-tolerant trees called mangroves form unusual coastal forests, growing with their roots partially underwater and their foliage above the water.

USA

CALIFORNIA

PACIFIC OCEAN

MEXICO

CALIFORNIA
USA

The Pacific Coast of North America is home to the world's biggest seaweed: giant kelp. In areas such as California, long strap-like fronds of giant kelp can reach 148 ft. (45 m) long and grow 24 in. (60 cm) per day!

SPONGES, MATS, AND COLONIES

The ocean animals most familiar to us have bodies that look and develop in predictable ways. But not all animals grow like this. The simplest kind of animals, called sponges, can grow in all sorts of ways, spreading out over the seafloor or growing branches like a plant.

INTRODUCING SPONGES

Chances are that the sponge in your bathroom is an artificial one, made from plastic. But there are similar-looking natural sponges that live in the ocean, too. Instead of plastic foam, natural sponges are made from a flexible organic substance called collagen. This is the same kind of material that helps your skin stay strong and supple.

It is thought that sea sponges have been used for bathing for around 3,000 years.

THE SIMPLEST ANIMALS

Sponges may look like plants, but they are actually the simplest animals on the planet today. They were among the first animals to evolve from single-celled organisms nearly a billion years ago. Their cells are only loosely connected. You could squeeze a sponge through a sieve, and the separated cells would then come back together and regrow to make a new sponge!

ALL SHAPES AND SIZES

In prehistoric seas, sponges grew into huge reefs, but these don't exist today. Instead, our reefs are made from a different kind of animal: coral. Sponges still exist, though, and in great diversity. Some have hard skeletons made from chalk or collagen. Others have delicate, glassy skeletons made from silica, which is also found in yellow sand.

Sea sponges provide shelter for small creatures, like reef fish.

A pair of shrimps may live their whole lives inside one Venus's flower basket sponge.

FINDING FOOD

Sponges grow in various ways, depending on the species. Some form creeping mats, while others look like upright vases or branching "trees." All contain special cells with beating, whip-like threads that drive currents of water into chambers inside the sponge. The cells that line these chambers filter out particles of food, which the sponge then feeds on.

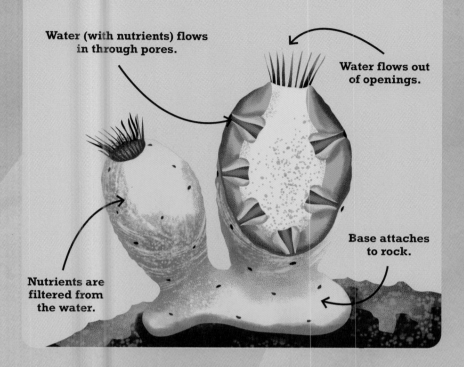

Water (with nutrients) flows in through pores.

Water flows out of openings.

Nutrients are filtered from the water.

Base attaches to rock.

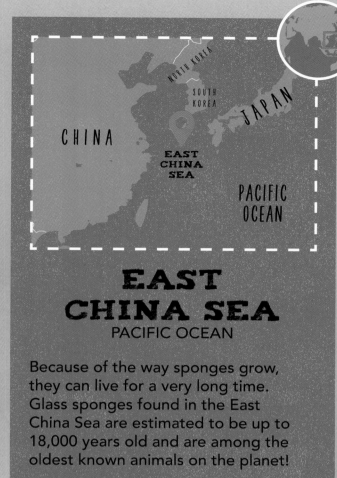

CHINA

NORTH KOREA

SOUTH KOREA

JAPAN

EAST CHINA SEA

PACIFIC OCEAN

EAST CHINA SEA
PACIFIC OCEAN

Because of the way sponges grow, they can live for a very long time. Glass sponges found in the East China Sea are estimated to be up to 18,000 years old and are among the oldest known animals on the planet!

COLONIAL ANIMALS

Sponges are colonial animals, meaning individual organisms live together to form a colony. Other animals have evolved to live like this, too. Bryozoans, or "moss animals," grow as creeping or tufted mats and filter-feed like sponges. Corals are also colonial animals, forming giant coral reefs (see pages 96–97).

A bryozoan is a colony of animals that have microscopic filter-feeding tentacles.

JELLIES AND ANEMONES

There isn't much to a jellyfish, apart from jelly! They have no heart, true eyes, or brain, and because they live underwater, jellyfish don't even need hard skeletons. Instead, their soft bodies are packed with water, which keeps them firm, and are supported by the water around them.

A WATER SKELETON

Water typically makes things squishy and flows from place to place, but when contained under pressure, it cannot be compressed (squashed). It therefore makes a surprisingly good skeleton, called a hydrostatic skeleton. (To test this, fill and seal a plastic bottle and then try to squeeze it.) A jellyfish may flop when it's on land, but in water, it keeps its shape even at bone-crushing depths.

The mauve stinger jellyfish is entirely covered in stingers.

The bell of a lion's mane jellyfish can grow over 6.5 ft. (2 m) wide – bigger than a human!

SWIMMING "BELLS"

Jellyfish were among the first animals to swim in the ocean half a billion years ago, and the jellyfish of today still share many of the same characteristics. A jellyfish has a single opening to its gut, which usually faces downward, between tentacles that hang from a pulsating "bell." And it has no brain – just a network of nerves running through the jelly of its body.

Bell

Tentacles

Opening to gut

Oral arms

DIFFERENT KINDS OF JELLYFISH

There are thousands of kinds of jellyfish. The biggest, called the lion's mane, drifts around the cold Arctic Ocean. Its trailing tentacles are the length of a school bus, and it can weigh a quarter of a ton. The smallest, with a "bell" no bigger than your thumbnail, is the Irukandji from tropical Australia. Both have stingers on their tentacles that can cause terrible pain.

JELLYFISH LAKE
PALAU

The island nation of Palau in the western Pacific is the location of a saltwater lake filled with thousands of golden jellyfish. Each day, the animals follow the path of the Sun as they migrate from one end of the lake to the other. The jellyfish contain photosynthesizing algae that help them make food. They have lost their ability to sting, so you can swim with them!

PALAU

PACIFIC OCEAN

INDONESIA

PAPUA NEW GUINEA

SIPHONOPHORES

Some creatures swim in open water and look like jellyfish but actually live in colonies, like coral. These are siphonophores. The Portuguese man-of-war, with its long dangling tentacles, is the most famous. It is topped with a gas-filled bag so it can float on the surface. Each siphonophore looks like a single jellyfish (they are closely related), but is really made up of a colony of polyps. Some polyps specialize in catching and eating prey, others are used to reproduce.

Many siphonophores can glow in the dark.

OCEAN STINGERS

Jellyfish use their stingers to stun or paralyze animal prey before they eat it. Their favorite foods are fish, crabs, shrimps, and even other types of jellyfish. Most are too mild to harm humans, but some, such as the wasp jellyfish, can give a nasty sting that can kill if left untreated – and it's practically invisible!

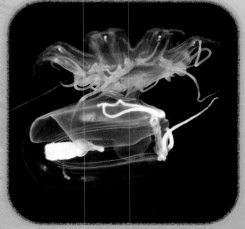

A jellyfish eats its paralyzed prey.

ANEMONES

Imagine a jellyfish lying upside down on the ocean bed with its tentacles wriggling upward. Does it look like an anemone? Anemones have similar stingers to jellyfish, but rather than swimming along, they stay fixed to the ocean bottom, where they wait for prey to swim past. Just the slightest touch will trigger the use of their stingers, which paralyze prey and guide it into the anemone's mouth.

Anemones have rings of tentacles around their mouths.

CORALS

A coral colony is made up of many tiny anemone-like animals called polyps, which are usually less than 0.6 in. (1.5 cm) across. Each polyp attaches itself to the rock and builds a hard, rock-like "cup" around itself (see pages 96–97). As a coral colony expands, these rocky structures build up in layers and can become as hard as the rock beneath. Over many years, rocky corals can grow to become a reef, like the Great Barrier Reef in Australia.

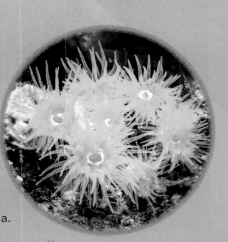

WORMS

The oceans are home to an enormous range of animal life, and some of these creatures behave in peculiar ways. Varieties of worms are common in the oceans, and although some look similar to the worms that live out of water, they live very different lives.

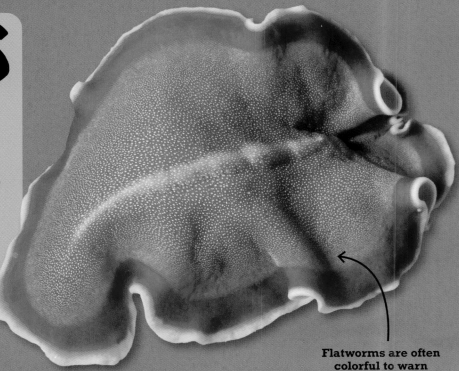

Flatworms are often colorful to warn off predators.

THE SIMPLEST WORMS

Flatworms are the simplest kinds of worms, and the simplest animals alive today with a head and a brain. Flatworms typically glide along the ocean bottom using a layer of microscopic beating hairs to propel themselves forward. Many flatworms in tropical coastal waters are brightly colored – a warning to predators that they could be poisonous.

SEGMENTED WORMS

The earthworms that you might find in garden soil have many ocean relatives, and both types have bodies divided into lots of similar parts, or segments. Many ocean segmented worms, such as predatory ragworms, have little flap-like paddles that help them grip as they wriggle over surfaces, whereas others are specialized for burrowing into the seabed.

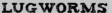

Some marine worms have hairy bristles that help them move about.

LUGWORMS

Sand and mud are important homes for burrowing segmented worms. They wriggle around, churning up the sediment and mixing life-giving oxygen into it. Lugworms live in a U-shaped burrow, with their rear end poking up toward one opening. At the bottom of the "U" they swallow mud, extract its nourishment, and then poop piles of waste sand that can be seen above the sandy surface!

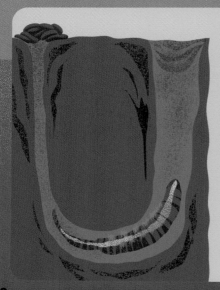

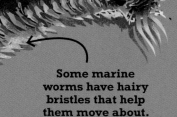

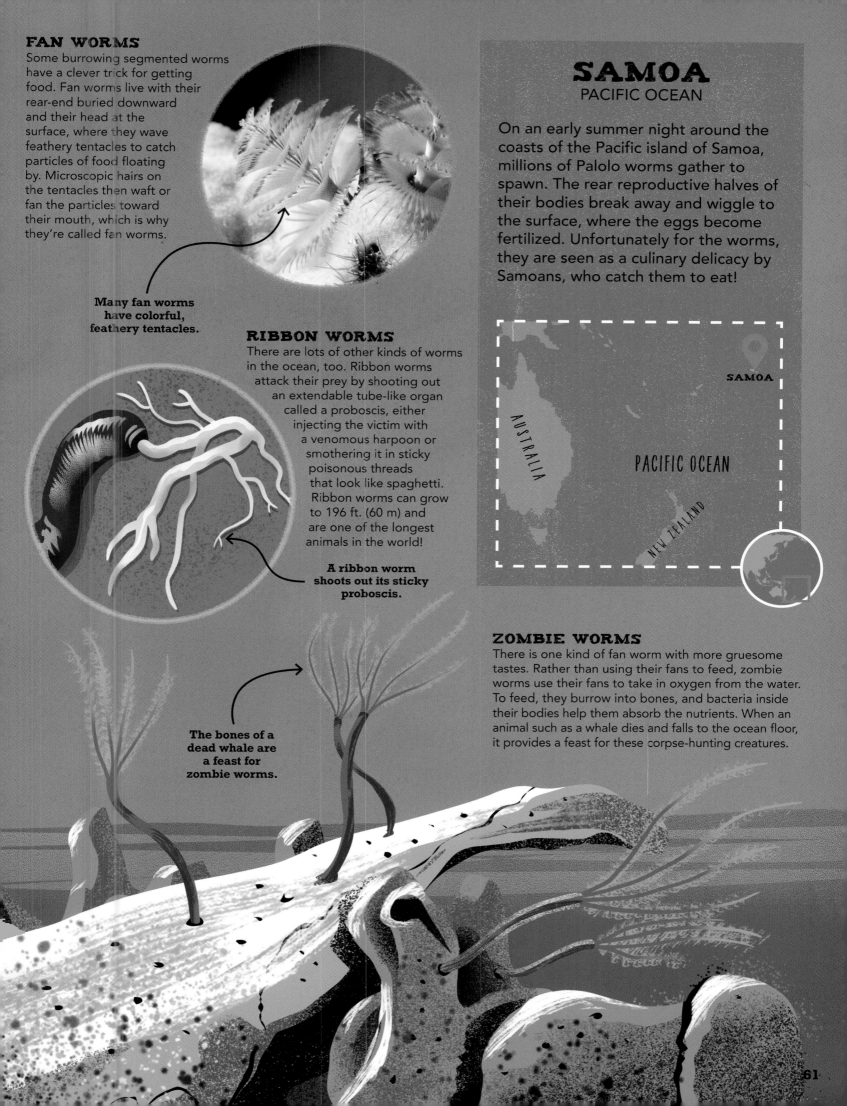

FAN WORMS

Some burrowing segmented worms have a clever trick for getting food. Fan worms live with their rear-end buried downward and their head at the surface, where they wave feathery tentacles to catch particles of food floating by. Microscopic hairs on the tentacles then waft or fan the particles toward their mouth, which is why they're called fan worms.

Many fan worms have colorful, feathery tentacles.

RIBBON WORMS

There are lots of other kinds of worms in the ocean, too. Ribbon worms attack their prey by shooting out an extendable tube-like organ called a proboscis, either injecting the victim with a venomous harpoon or smothering it in sticky poisonous threads that look like spaghetti. Ribbon worms can grow to 196 ft. (60 m) and are one of the longest animals in the world!

A ribbon worm shoots out its sticky proboscis.

SAMOA
PACIFIC OCEAN

On an early summer night around the coasts of the Pacific island of Samoa, millions of Palolo worms gather to spawn. The rear reproductive halves of their bodies break away and wiggle to the surface, where the eggs become fertilized. Unfortunately for the worms, they are seen as a culinary delicacy by Samoans, who catch them to eat!

SAMOA

AUSTRALIA

PACIFIC OCEAN

NEW ZEALAND

ZOMBIE WORMS

There is one kind of fan worm with more gruesome tastes. Rather than using their fans to feed, zombie worms use their fans to take in oxygen from the water. To feed, they burrow into bones, and bacteria inside their bodies help them absorb the nutrients. When an animal such as a whale dies and falls to the ocean floor, it provides a feast for these corpse-hunting creatures.

The bones of a dead whale are a feast for zombie worms.

61

MOLLUSKS

A lot of animals in the ocean are described as shellfish but, despite the name, they are not actually fish. Shellfish are invertebrates (animals without a backbone) with shells or tough body armor for protection. Among them are mollusks, including limpets, snails, and clams. There are also mollusks without shells, such as slugs and octopuses.

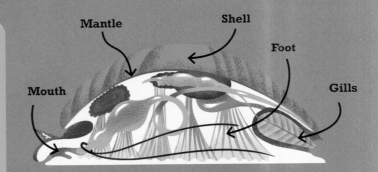

Mantle Shell Foot Mouth Gills

WHAT IS A MOLLUSK?

All mollusks have soft bodies and just one big foot, which can be almost as big as their entire body! Mollusks are covered in a layer of skin called a mantle. The mantle hangs over the edge of the body and is usually where gills for breathing underwater are found. The mantle of limpets and snails also produces a hard shell.

Giant squid can grow up to 43 ft. (13 m) long!

In 2004, divers filmed a giant squid in its natural habitat for the very first time.

SHELLS OF DIFFERENT SHAPES

There are tens of thousands of kinds of mollusks, and they produce shells in a huge range of shapes. Some, like limpets, have simple conical caps, like a pointed hat. Others, such as periwinkles and whelks, have shells that twist into a coil as they grow. These animals can hide deep inside their shells for protection. Some snails can even seal the entrance with a "trapdoor" called an operculum.

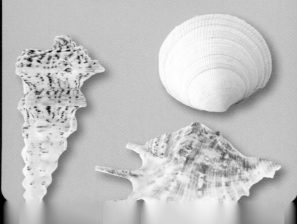

GRAZERS AND PREDATORS

Limpets and snails creep along on a single muscular foot and feed using a tongue-like structure called a radula. The radula of a limpet is coated in tiny teeth hardened with iron, making them strong enough to scrape algae from rocks, even leaving scratches in the process. Some other snails, such as whelks, are predators and have a beak-like radula for boring into the shells of prey, including barnacles and even other snails.

Lots of ocean-living snails have lost their shells through evolution. These shell-less snails are called sea slugs but are unrelated to slugs that live on land. Some sea slugs have tufts on their backs that contain stinging cells stolen from their prey; instead of digesting venom, they collect it and use it for defense. Sea slugs are often brightly colored as a warning.

BIVALVES

One group of mollusks, called bivalves, have shells made of two parts that are hinged in the middle. Special muscles allow the bivalve to open and shut its shell. With an open shell, it uses its gills or tentacles to trap particles of food. If danger is near, the animal quickly closes its shell and holds it tightly shut.

CEPHALOPODS

The fastest moving, smartest mollusks of all are squid and octopuses. They are called cephalopods, meaning "head-footed," and have evolved tentacles from their single foot. A nautilus has more arms than any other cephalopod – males have around 90! Octopuses are among the strangest of the cephalopods. They can shoot out dark ink when startled and even lose an arm to escape the grasp of a predator – which they can grow back later!

An octopus releases ink when threatened and makes a swift getaway.

INTELLIGENT PREDATORS

Cephalopods have well-developed brains, making them smart. There is one species of squid bigger than the giant squid (above), and they are among the most feared predators in the ocean: the colossal squid. At an intimidating 46 ft. (14 m) long, the mysterious colossal squid dwells in deep ocean waters and is the largest known invertebrate animal of all. It has curved hooks on its tentacles, which it uses to attack huge prey. Many sperm whales have scars from colossal squid attacks!

Giant squid live in deep water and are extremely rare.

CRUSTACEANS

Many crustaceans are types of shellfish, including shrimps and crabs. They wear their skeletons on the outside of their bodies, and this tough outer casing is called an exoskeleton. Just like insects and spiders (which they're related to), crustaceans have flexible, multi-jointed legs. Crustaceans are abundant in the oceans and there are tens of thousands of different species.

Krill swarms can get so big that they are seen from space!

A hermit crab "moves shell" when it grows big enough.

CRABS

Crabs are "decapod" crustaceans, which means they have 10 legs, with the front pair used as pincers for warding off attackers or grabbing food. Some crabs are tiny and others grow into giants. Unlike true crabs, the soft-bodied hermit crab doesn't grow its own protective shell. Instead, it borrows the empty shells of snails, and as it grows, it finds a bigger shell to match its new size.

ARMORED GIANTS

Ocean crustaceans can grow much bigger than insects on land. The American lobster weighs up to 44 lb. (20 kg), and the Japanese spider crab has a leg span of more than 16 ft. (5 m)! These are the biggest crustaceans of them all and are thought to live up to 100 years old.

CRUSTACEAN BODY PARTS

Just like insects, a crustacean's body can be divided into three parts: a head, thorax, and abdomen. Most kinds of crustaceans look like shrimps with long, segmented bodies and pairs of multi-jointed legs that give them lots of flexibility. Some species, like crabs and lobsters, have a pair of powerful claws, which they use for self-defense and to gather food.

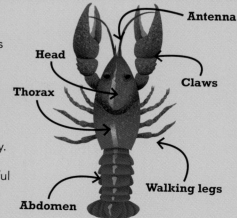

Antenna

Head

Thorax

Claws

Walking legs

Abdomen

CRAYFISH

NEW ARMOR FOR OLD

Back-boned animals (like humans) have their skeleton on the inside, and the bones grow with their body. But in crustaceans, the exoskeleton works more like a suit of armor. When a crab or shrimp grows, a new bigger exoskeleton grows beneath the old one. The old exoskeleton is then shed during a molt.

A new exoskeleton develops beneath the old one.

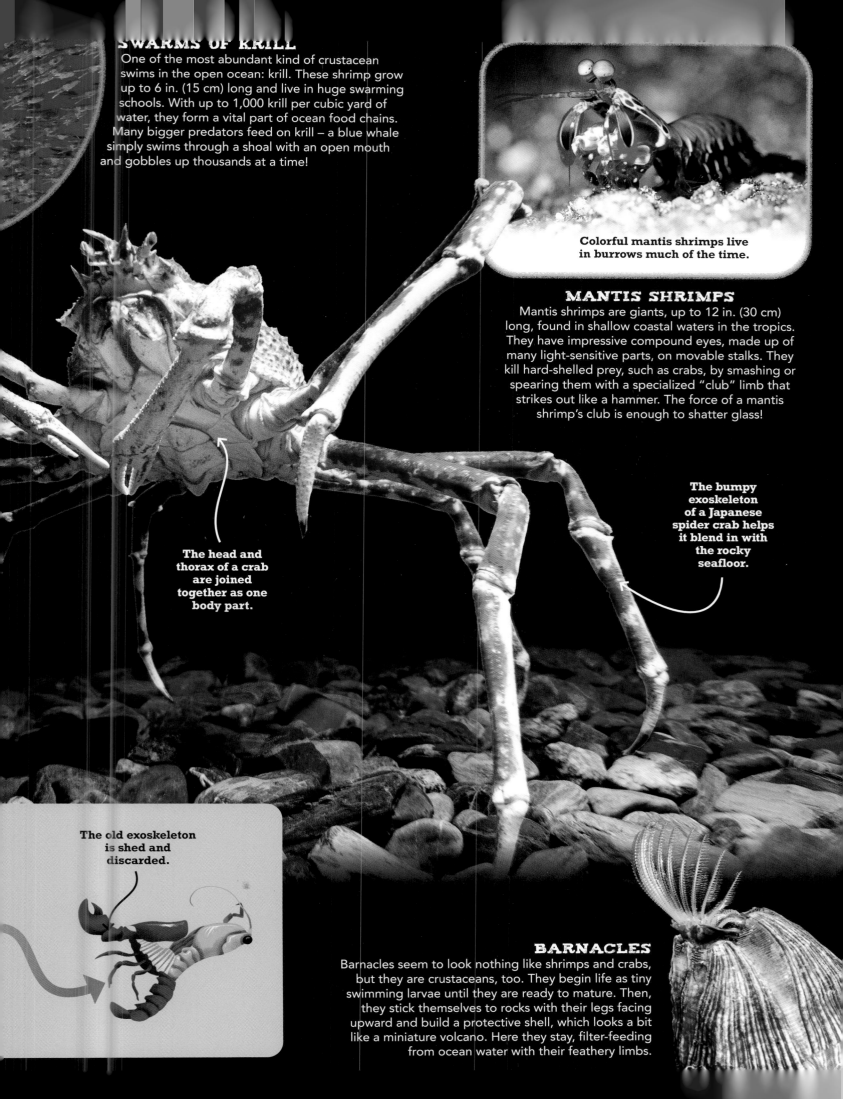

SWARMS OF KRILL

One of the most abundant kind of crustacean swims in the open ocean: krill. These shrimp grow up to 6 in. (15 cm) long and live in huge swarming schools. With up to 1,000 krill per cubic yard of water, they form a vital part of ocean food chains. Many bigger predators feed on krill – a blue whale simply swims through a shoal with an open mouth and gobbles up thousands at a time!

Colorful mantis shrimps live in burrows much of the time.

MANTIS SHRIMPS

Mantis shrimps are giants, up to 12 in. (30 cm) long, found in shallow coastal waters in the tropics. They have impressive compound eyes, made up of many light-sensitive parts, on movable stalks. They kill hard-shelled prey, such as crabs, by smashing or spearing them with a specialized "club" limb that strikes out like a hammer. The force of a mantis shrimp's club is enough to shatter glass!

The bumpy exoskeleton of a Japanese spider crab helps it blend in with the rocky seafloor.

The head and thorax of a crab are joined together as one body part.

The old exoskeleton is shed and discarded.

BARNACLES

Barnacles seem to look nothing like shrimps and crabs, but they are crustaceans, too. They begin life as tiny swimming larvae until they are ready to mature. Then, they stick themselves to rocks with their legs facing upward and build a protective shell, which looks a bit like a miniature volcano. Here they stay, filter-feeding from ocean water with their feathery limbs.

SPINY-SKINNED ECHINODERMS

Echinoderms, such as starfish and sea urchins, are the only big animal group that lives purely in the oceans – none have adapted to live in rivers or on land. Their bodies typically look like stars, with arms or body sections arranged around a central point and a mouth in the middle. Many echinoderms can regrow parts of their body if they are lost or damaged.

The skin of an urchin is made of tough, flexible plates.

SKIN SKELETON

"Echinoderm" means "spiny-skinned." A unique feature of these creatures is that they have hard parts of their skeleton embedded within their skin. In sea urchins, these form plates that lock together to make a shell, but in starfish, the skeleton parts are separate plates that work like tiny joints, making the animal more flexible.

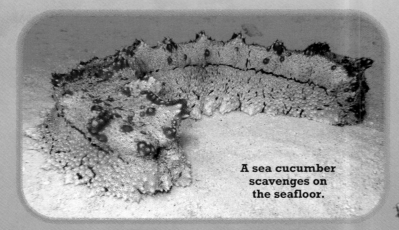

A sea cucumber scavenges on the seafloor.

STARFISH

Most starfish have five arms that stretch out from the center, but some kinds have more. Many are predators of slow-moving prey and are experts at opening shells. They hunt down creatures like mussels, grip their victim with their arms, and pull open the shell. Then they shoot their flexible stomach out through their mouths to digest their prey.

Starfish have tiny tube feet that help them grip to rocks and move over rough surfaces.

SEA CUCUMBERS

Sea cucumbers look less like starfish and more like big sausages, with rows of tube feet beneath them and a mouth at one end. They have a skeletal system made of individual crystal particles that work together to toughen the skin. Sea cucumbers play an important role as the ocean's cleaners – vacuuming up and eating decaying organic matter from the sea bottom.

SEA URCHINS

Most sea urchins are grazers, using hard jaws to bite away at any seaweed or coral in their path. Urchins have a coating of sharp spines and some are venomous, but they use their spines for self-defense rather than to attack prey. Like other echinoderms, urchins creep along on hundreds of fleshy rod-like feet, called tube feet, that move by a system that involves seawater circulating through the body.

BRITTLE STARS

Some of the fastest-moving echinoderms are brittle stars. They have a similar multi-armed body to starfish, but their arms are thinner and more flexible. Instead of creeping along on tube feet, they crawl around using their wriggling arms, scavenging particles of food.

PUGET SOUND
WASHINGTON, USA

The world's largest starfish lives around Puget Sound on the western coast of the US. The sunflower sea star reaches up to 3.3 ft. (1 m) in diameter and can have 24 arms! But populations of this ocean giant have crashed in recent years as a result of global warming.

CANADA

PACIFIC OCEAN

PUGET SOUND

USA

FEATHER STARS

Filter-feeding feather stars sit on the ocean bed with their mouths facing upward toward the surface. They wave their feathery arms in the water currents to trap particles of food – a bit like an anemone with its feeding tentacles. Sea lilies are also connected to the seabed by a stalk and look like colorful underwater flowers.

THE POWER OF REGENERATION

Slow-moving echinoderms might seem vulnerable to predators, but starfish can grow back lost arms when injured and some can even regenerate an entire body from just a portion of a severed limb. Sea cucumbers benefit from the power of regeneration in another way – they can explode their guts in a sticky mess into the face of an attacker, and then grow them back afterward!

Feather stars are colorful inhabitants of the seabed.

A starfish can grow a new body from a lost leg.

SHARKS AND RAYS

There are over 500 species of sharks and 600 species of rays swimming in the oceans, from the hand-sized dwarf shark to the giant whale shark. Unlike most vertebrates (back-boned animals), sharks and rays have skeletons made from a rubbery material called cartilage. This makes them more lightweight than fish with bony skeletons.

The great white shark is a fearsome hunter.

LIGHTEN UP

A skeleton made from cartilage is about half as dense as one made from bone, so it doesn't weigh the body down as much. Predatory sharks and rays also have oil in their flesh that adds to their buoyancy – without this they could still sink! Most sharks have a long torpedo-shaped body propelled by a thrashing tail.

The whale shark is about the length of a school bus!

OCEAN PREDATORS

All sharks prey on other animals – but their preference varies enormously. Great white sharks are speedy hunters that can kill warm-blooded prey, such as seals. Basking sharks and whale sharks cruise along with their mouths gaping wide to strain smaller creatures such as planktonic krill.

GIANT FILTER FEEDERS

Basking sharks, megamouth sharks, and whale sharks are filter-feeders, using special filters in their enormous mouths to extract floating plankton in the open water. The whale shark is the biggest living fish of all, sometimes reaching lengths of over 66 ft. (20 m) with a mouth that can be around 5 ft. (1.5 m) wide.

The gaping mouth of a basking shark.

The wide-set eyes of a hammerhead shark give it a better visual range.

SENSING PREY

Sharks and rays are armed with very sharp senses to help them track prey, making them top predators. Their heads are dotted with tiny jelly-filled pits that detect the electrical signals coming from muscles and nerves of other animals. There's nowhere to hide from hammerhead sharks – they use the sensors in their wide heads to find prey even when it's buried under the sand!

GRAB A BITE

Being a meat-eater in deeper ocean waters poses a challenge – there isn't much meat to go around. Cookiecutter sharks have a cunning plan: they swim close to a whale or another shark, then dart in to gouge out a circular mouthful of flesh! Their razor-sharp teeth are the biggest in proportion to their body size of any shark.

The parasitic cookiecutter shark feeds off live animals.

The mako shark can swim at 25 mph (40 kph).

HOT-BLOODED HUNTERS

Some sharks have a special adaptation for chasing down prey – they generate heat from muscles to make them partially warm-blooded. This improves their stamina, making them more than a match for other warm-blooded targets, like mammals and birds. It turns great white sharks (the biggest flesh-eating sharks) and mako sharks (the fastest sharks) into fearsome ocean hunters.

Manta rays filter-feed on plankton.

MASTERS OF AMBUSH

Some sharks have the perfect disguise to ambush passing prey. Wobbegongs have a flat, ray-like body that blends in with the seabed, but they are quick to grab anything that comes close to their wide, sharp-toothed mouths. In polar seas, the Greenland shark may appear slow – until it creeps up on unsuspecting seals and seabirds, snatching them from floating ice.

The spotted skin of a wobbegong acts as camouflage against the muddy ocean floor.

GIANT RAYS

Most rays and skates spend much of their time on the sea bottom, where they scavenge for buried food, like hiding crabs and clams. The biggest species live in the open water and are graceful swimmers. Manta rays are the biggest rays of all – they can grow up to 23 ft. (7 m) wide from wing tip to wing tip and live up to 50 years!

NINGALOO REEF
AUSTRALIA

Ningaloo Reef, off the west coast of Australia, is one of the best places in the world to see whale sharks. Visitors can even snorkel with the sharks! These ocean giants arrive in April to fill up on krill and plankton drawn to the reef by a mass coral spawning.

NINGALOO REEF

AUSTRALIA

THE FIRST BONY FISH

There are over 34,000 different species of bony fish, making it the most diverse group of back-boned animals alive today. It is also one of the oldest, with fossils up to 420 million years old! Bony fish live in nearly all water habitats but the vast majority live in the ocean – from the coastal shallows to the ocean bottom.

COELACANTHS

In 1938, a fleshy-finned fish was caught off the coast of South Africa that was thought to have gone extinct with the dinosaurs around 65 million years ago! Coelacanths are related to the first fish that evolved into land-living amphibians. The species may have existed for 360 million years, giving it the name "living fossil." They usually hide in dark underwater caverns in the Indian Ocean.

Coelacanths are related to fish that lived millions of years ago and are rarely seen.

STURGEONS

Despite being related to fish with bony skeletons, sturgeons have rubbery skeletons made from cartilage – just like sharks. Most species live in estuaries or coastal waters but migrate into rivers to spawn. Migratory fish like this adapt their bodies by regulating the amount of sodium they take in from the water, so they can survive in both saltwater and freshwater.

DRAGONFISH OF THE DEEP

Many families of fish contain species that live in the deep sea, including dragonfish and deep-sea lizardfish. With soft water-filled bodies, deep-sea fish are better adapted to cope with the higher pressure, and can live in depths of up to 7,874 ft. (2,400 m)! Food is scarce down here, so many of these fish have larger mouths to give them a greater chance of catching any prey that swims nearby.

Deep-sea lizardfish hunt at extreme depths.

Giant moray eels are found all over the world.

EELS

Freshwater eels migrate to the open ocean to spawn, but most kinds of eels live permanently in the ocean. Colorful moray eels hunt around coral reefs, hiding in caves and crevices. They grasp prey with their powerful jaws, then another hidden set of jaws inside the eel's throat grabs the food and drags it back to be swallowed. An eel's backbone has around 100 small bones called vertebrae, which makes it very flexible. Humans only have 33.

A shoal of fish that swims together in a coordinated way is called a "school."

AGULHAS BANK
SOUTH AFRICA

Each year, from May to July, billions of South African pilchards (also called sardines) spawn in the Agulhas Bank and then migrate up the east coast of Africa in what has become known as the "Sardine Run." As billions of darting sardines move northward, they are preyed on by hungry sharks and whales that take advantage of the feast.

NAMIBIA
BOTSWANA
LESOTHO
SOUTH AFRICA
SOUTH ATLANTIC OCEAN
AGULHAS BANK

SHOALS AND SCHOOLS
Many fish, such as herring and bigeye trevally (above), gather into huge shoals – a tactic that improves individual chances of survival. When shoals of fish swim together in a coordinated way, the group is called a "school." Fish decide how to move based on the movement of other fish around them, so they need to be ultra-sensitive to tiny changes in speed and direction.

BONY FISH EVOLVE

The most advanced bony fish have hollow spines on the fin running down their back. These fish have evolved to live in practically every ocean habitat, and include colorful fish of tropical reefs, mysterious deep-sea fish, and many other varieties that swim in shoals in the open ocean.

GOBIES AND BLENNIES

Some fish, such as gobies and blennies, have fins that are specially adapted for clinging to rocks, which stops them from being swept away by coastal waves. One group of gobies, called mudskippers, can use their fins to "walk" and even "dance" on mud at low tide – all to attract a mate! Water held in their gill chambers allows them to breathe on land.

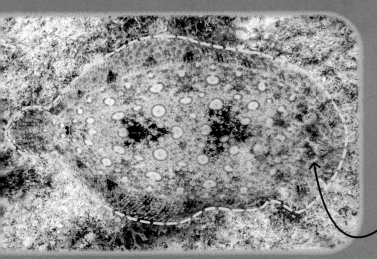

FLATFISH

Flatfish have a strange way of maturing. While they are young, they look like most fish with one eye either side of their head. But as they age, they go through a metamorphosis (bodily change), when one eye moves next to the other, making them blind on one side. Mature fish settle on the seabed with both eyes facing upward and their body camouflaged to match the sand.

Even the eyes of a flatfish can blend into the seafloor!

ATAURO ISLAND
EAST TIMOR

When conservationists studied the waters around Atauro Island in East Timor, between Asia and Australia, they found this location to have the highest diversity of reef fish anywhere in the world. They found an average of 253 species per site that was surveyed and a total of 642 species around the entire island.

INDONESIA

ATAURO
ISLAND

INDIAN
OCEAN

AUSTRALIA

VENOMOUS FISH

Some fish rely on poisons to help them survive. Pufferfish have poisons in their flesh that make them nasty tasting, or even dangerous to eat. Other fish use venom that is injected into the skin of an attacker through spines that line their backs. Scorpionfish, stonefish, and lionfish can deliver excruciatingly painful stings when grabbed by a predator.

ANGLERFISH

It might not be the prettiest fish, but it has a clever way to bait its prey. An anglerfish can be recognized by the lure that hangs like a rod above its gaping mouth. In some species that hunt in the dark depths, the lure lights up to attract prey to its toothy mouth. An anglerfish can even swallow prey up to twice its own size!

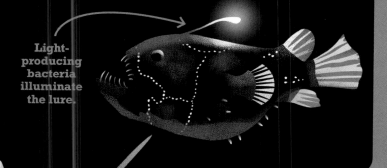

Light-producing bacteria illuminate the lure.

SEAHORSES

These slow, shallow-water fish are propelled by their rippling dorsal (back) fin, which flutters up to 35 times per second. They are masters of disguise, able to coil their armored tails around weeds or coral and even change color to match their environment so that predators don't spot them. Seahorses mate for life and can be seen swimming in pairs with their tails entwined when trying to win the affection of the other.

Seahorses use their tails to grip onto seaweed, or a mate!

Lionfish have beautiful but venomous spines.

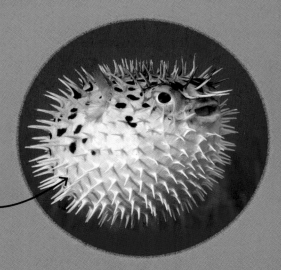

Pufferfish are extremely poisonous.

PUFFERFISH

Threatening behavior can be the best defense for some fish. Pufferfish have a strategy that makes them swell to several times their usual size — by swallowing huge amounts of seawater (which they later release to deflate). While inflated, they look like large, spiky balls and are too big to fit into the mouths of many ocean predators!

Young emperor angelfish

DEVELOPING PATTERNS

Fish of the tropical ocean reefs are among the most colorful animals on the planet. Different patterns help species to recognize each other and to find a mate. Many reef fish, such as angelfish, develop different patterns as they mature. Some fish can even change sex (and therefore pattern) if necessary. A school of adult clownfish are nearly all male, apart from one female fish. When the female dies, the most dominant male changes sex, and pattern, to replace her.

Adult emperor angelfish

VISITORS FROM THE LAND

Some organisms, such as seaweed, crabs, and fish, originally evolved to live in the ocean, and most kinds have stayed there ever since. Other groups of living things now live in the ocean but have ancestors that originally lived on land. Many of these are temporary visitors that use the ocean as a source of food.

An Adélie penguin sits on its eggs for 30–40 days.

INSECTS

Insects are one of the most diverse groups of living things on land – dominating the natural, air-breathing world. But very few insects can tolerate saltwater, so they tend to stay away from the oceans. The few that do venture near the waves, including beetles and flies, stick to seashore habitats, where they feed among seaweed and other detritus thrown up by the tide.

Salt creek tiger beetles burrow in mudflats and seal their entrances at high tide.

MARINE IGUANAS

Only one species of lizard gets its food entirely from the ocean. The marine iguana from the Galápagos Islands dives into the cold waters to graze on seaweed just below the surface, before quickly returning to land to warm up its chilled body under the heat of the tropical sun.

The saltwater crocodile sleeps with one eye open!

SALTWATER CROCODILE

Most crocodilians (a group of reptiles that includes crocodiles and alligators) are freshwater animals, but a couple of species venture into coastal waters. The saltwater crocodile is the world's largest living reptile and regularly visits the oceans. Its high salt tolerance means it can swim far away from land and has colonized many islands between Asia and Australia.

WHAT KEEPS LAND ANIMALS ON LAND?

Crustaceans and fish can breathe and breed underwater – they have gills to extract oxygen from water and produce soft eggs or swimming larvae as young. But many air-breathing animals, such as reptiles and birds, lay hard-shelled eggs that need to be surrounded by air to develop properly, so they can only breed on land.

Rock pipits forage for food between rocks.

Sea otters use rocks to crack the shells of their prey.

BIRDS

The ocean and the seashore can be a rich food supply for birds, from flitting rock pipits to round, flightless kiwis. They visit the seashore to pick among seaweed, looking for beetles, insects, and shellfish. Others wade out into mud to probe for worms and other buried invertebrates. Some go even further, diving into the water to fish for a meal and bringing it ashore to eat.

MAMMALS

Lots of mammals take the plunge, too. Sea otters dive for mollusks like clams in underwater kelp forests, and all around the world seals and sea lions dive for fish. These carnivores have flipper-like limbs for swimming, but still have the ability to haul themselves onto the land, where they stay to give birth.

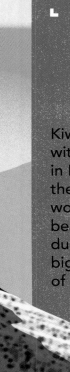

Marine iguanas warm themselves up by sunbathing.

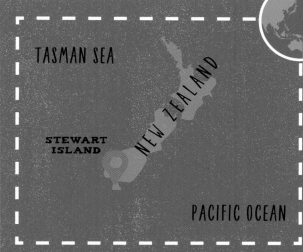

TASMAN SEA

NEW ZEALAND

STEWART ISLAND

PACIFIC OCEAN

STEWART ISLAND
NEW ZEALAND

Kiwis are birds that usually stay within forests, but on Stewart Island in New Zealand, they venture out of the undergrowth at night to pick up worms and small crayfish on the sandy beaches. Kiwis are nocturnal and sleep during the day. They lay impressively big eggs that can be up to a quarter of an adult bird's body weight!

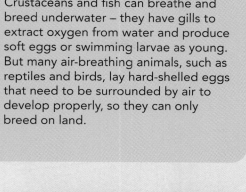

OCEANIC REPTILES

Some reptiles have adapted so well to life in the oceans that they spend almost all their lives there, only coming to land to lay their hard-shelled eggs. They are really as much a part of the permanent ocean community as coral and fish.

Loggerhead turtles use their strong jaws to crush hard prey.

MARINE TURTLES

Turtles and tortoises are reptiles with much of their body protected by a hard shell. Most kinds, even those turtles that live in freshwater rivers and ponds, walk on clawed feet. But ocean-going sea turtles have flippers instead of claws, making them better adapted for life in the water.

HOW MARINE TURTLES BREED

All marine turtles feed, socialize, and mate in the ocean, but pregnant females lay their eggs on the shore. They use their flippers to haul themselves onto sandy beaches – often traveling huge distances to return to the same beach where they themselves hatched. They dig a pit for their eggs, then cover them with sand where they incubate (develop in their shells) using the Sun's warmth.

Pregnant turtles travel ashore to lay their eggs.

Marine turtles usually lay over 100 eggs in one nest!

SEA KRAITS

Some venomous snakes of the cobra-mamba family have evolved to swim in the ocean, and even have paddle-shaped tails to help them get around. These snakes use their powerful venom to prey on cold-blooded creatures, such as fish. Sea kraits only feed at night and, like turtles, must come ashore to lay hard-shelled eggs.

Sea kraits are amphibious and move from water to land.

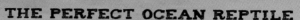

Sea snakes can also breathe through their skin.

THE PERFECT OCEAN REPTILE

True sea snakes, unlike sea kraits, are the best adapted reptiles for life underwater. Like all reptiles, they still have to come to the surface to breathe, but they no longer lay their eggs on land. Instead, they give birth to live young in the ocean. They are highly venomous and can grow to over 6.5 ft. (2 m) long, but are not aggressive toward humans.

Many species of sea turtles are critically endangered and threatened by human actions, including plastic pollution.

ATLANTIC OCEAN

TRINIDAD

VENEZUELA

COLOMBIA

GUYANA

TURTLES IN THE OCEAN

Once hatched, turtles dig themselves out of the sand and race urgently to the ocean, before land predators such as gulls and foxes can catch them. No one knows for sure where they go, but they're amazing navigators and travel thousands of miles during their lifetimes. Adult green turtles return to coastal waters to graze, while others, such as the giant leatherback, stay in the open ocean. Some turtles can live up to 150 years!

TRINIDAD
SOUTH AMERICA

The protected sandy beaches of Trinidad in the Caribbean are among the most important nesting sites of the leatherback turtle – the largest species of turtle. Each year, more than 10,000 turtles arrive to lay their eggs. Because a turtle's sex is determined by the temperature of the sand in which it develops, climate change is causing a population imbalance, with more females being born than males.

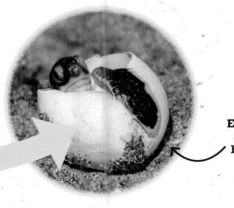

Eggs incubate for around 60 days before hatching.

OCEAN MAMMALS

Two groups of mammals are so well adapted to life in water that they can no longer return to the land at all. These are cetaceans, which include dolphins and whales, and sirenians, such as manatees and dugongs. Both groups give birth underwater and only rise to the surface to take big breaths of air, before ducking back down beneath the waves.

Although they're sometimes called killer whales, orcas are actually a giant kind of dolphin that has evolved to feed on bigger prey, such as seals.

Fluke

Blowhole

Flippers

BUILT FOR WATER

Cetaceans are perfectly adapted for living underwater. Dolphins and whales have long streamlined bodies and smooth hairless skin, which makes them glide easily through water. They have a wide horizontal tail fin, known as a fluke, that flaps up and down, pushing them forward. Their front limbs are flippers for steering and they have a blowhole at the top of the head for breathing.

Dolphins are sociable animals that hunt in groups called "pods."

DOLPHINS

There are around 40 different species of dolphins, the most of any cetacean, and they are found almost everywhere in the world. Some prefer coastal waters and others live further out at sea. To locate fish and other prey in the murky depths, dolphins make clicking noises and listen to how the sound echoes back to them. This is called echolocation. They have long beak-like jaws armed with teeth to catch their prey.

Sperm whales and giant squid are thought to battle deep in the ocean.

GIANT PREDATORS

The biggest toothed cetacean is the sperm whale (the blue whale is bigger but it doesn't have teeth). Sperm whales dive to depths of over 6,500 ft. (2,000 m), preying on the elusive giant squid. They have the biggest brains on the planet – about six times heavier than a human brain.

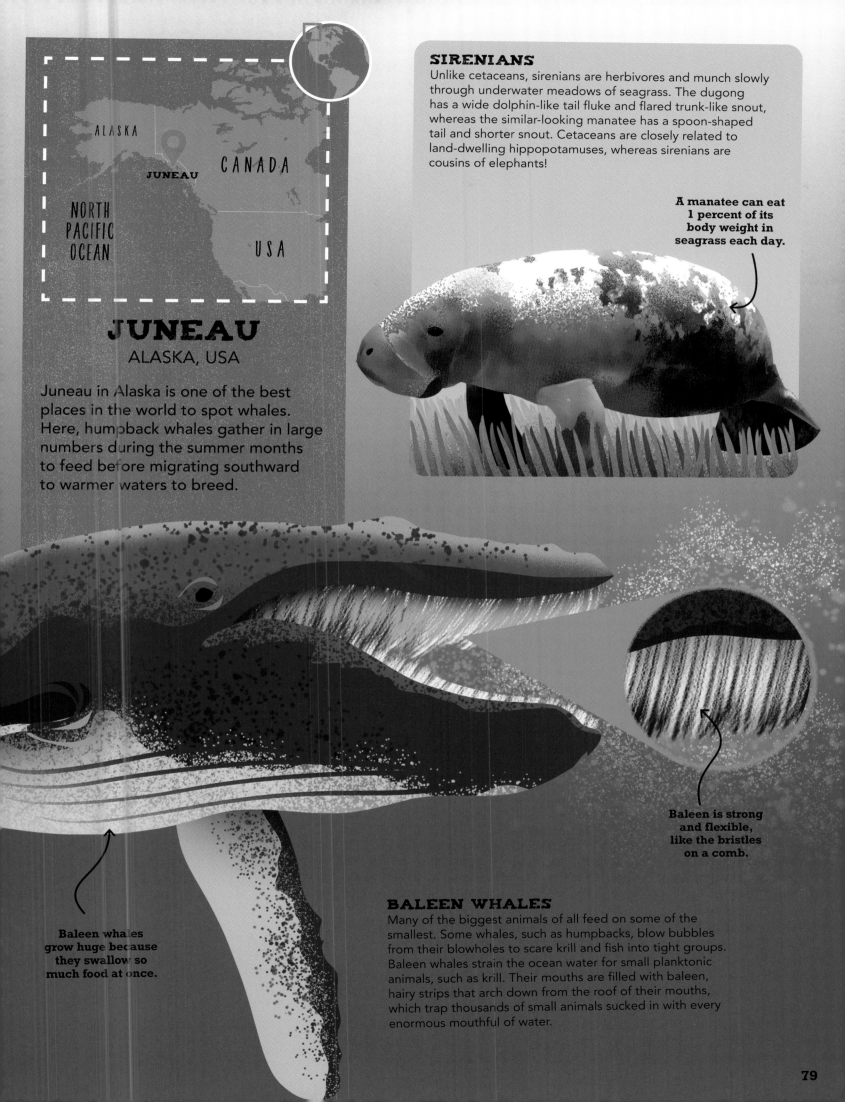

SIRENIANS

Unlike cetaceans, sirenians are herbivores and munch slowly through underwater meadows of seagrass. The dugong has a wide dolphin-like tail fluke and flared trunk-like snout, whereas the similar-looking manatee has a spoon-shaped tail and shorter snout. Cetaceans are closely related to land-dwelling hippopotamuses, whereas sirenians are cousins of elephants!

A manatee can eat 1 percent of its body weight in seagrass each day.

ALASKA

JUNEAU

CANADA

NORTH PACIFIC OCEAN

USA

JUNEAU
ALASKA, USA

Juneau in Alaska is one of the best places in the world to spot whales. Here, humpback whales gather in large numbers during the summer months to feed before migrating southward to warmer waters to breed.

Baleen is strong and flexible, like the bristles on a comb.

Baleen whales grow huge because they swallow so much food at once.

BALEEN WHALES

Many of the biggest animals of all feed on some of the smallest. Some whales, such as humpbacks, blow bubbles from their blowholes to scare krill and fish into tight groups. Baleen whales strain the ocean water for small planktonic animals, such as krill. Their mouths are filled with baleen, hairy strips that arch down from the roof of their mouths, which trap thousands of small animals sucked in with every enormous mouthful of water.

OCEANIC BIRDS

There are over 10,000 species of birds, but none of these live permanently in the ocean. All seabirds have to come to shore to lay their eggs and breed. Even so, many birds spend much of their time at sea hunting for food, and some are entirely dependent upon the oceans for their survival.

LONG-DISTANCE GLIDERS

Albatrosses and shearwaters probably spend more time flying over the ocean than any other kind of bird. They use their long wings to ride the air currents by gliding, which saves energy needed for flapping. Unlike most birds, they have a good sense of smell, helping them to track fishy prey over long distances.

An albatross can fly 9,942 mi. (16,000 km) in one journey.

FISHING FROM THE AIR

For birds with good flying skills, one way to grab a meal is to dive into the water from the air. Gannets, boobies, and brown pelicans are all impressive divers, plunging straight downward into shoals of fish near the ocean surface to grab prey, before turning skyward again.

Gannets dive for fish near Auckland, New Zealand.

Godwits use their long bills to probe the mud.

Sheathbills are scavengers, even eating dead penguins.

MUD-PROBING WADERS

Sandpipers and similar birds, such as godwits, plovers, and curlews, depend on coastal mud and sediment for food, especially during winter. They probe for buried worms and other invertebrates with their bills. Some have longer legs for wading into deeper waters, or longer bills to probe deeper into the mud. During summer, many of these birds move inland to breed in meadows and marshland.

THE OPPORTUNISTS

Some waders, such as gulls, are not at all fussy about where they get their next meal. Many gulls are just as at home scavenging inland as they are at snatching fish from the sea. Around Antarctica, sheathbills will eat anything that they find, from other birds' eggs to scraps of flesh, and even other animals' poop.

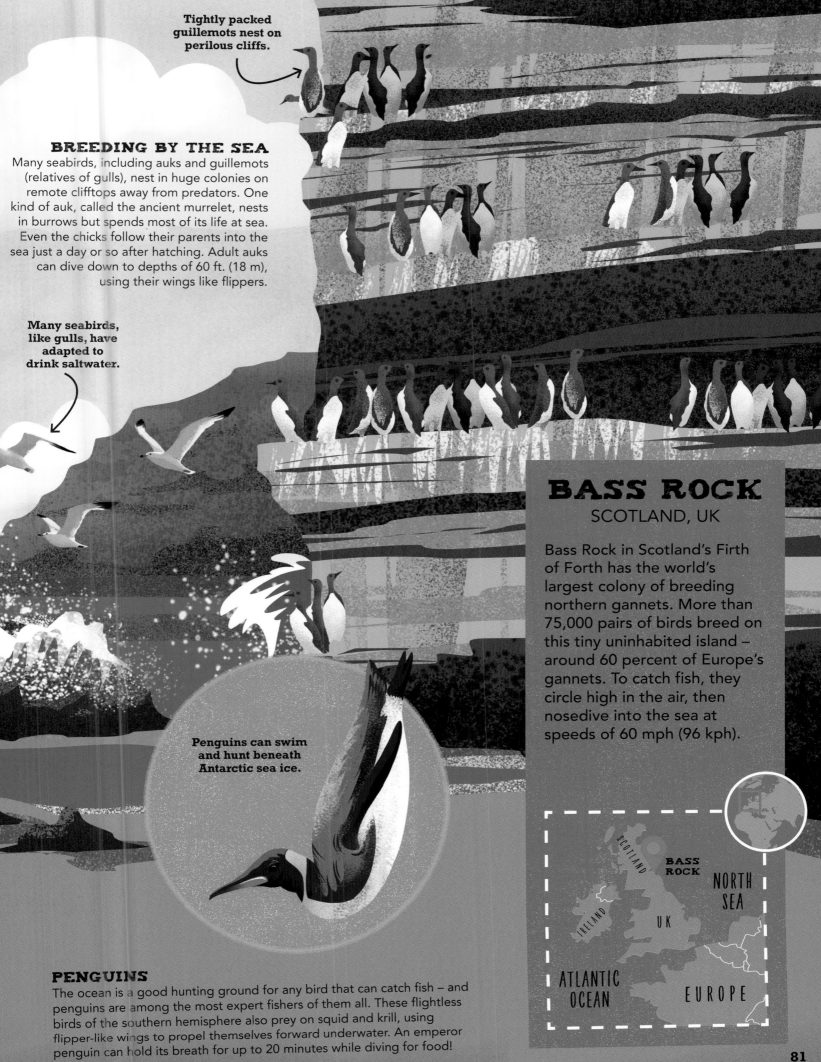

Tightly packed guillemots nest on perilous cliffs.

BREEDING BY THE SEA

Many seabirds, including auks and guillemots (relatives of gulls), nest in huge colonies on remote clifftops away from predators. One kind of auk, called the ancient murrelet, nests in burrows but spends most of its life at sea. Even the chicks follow their parents into the sea just a day or so after hatching. Adult auks can dive down to depths of 60 ft. (18 m), using their wings like flippers.

Many seabirds, like gulls, have adapted to drink saltwater.

Penguins can swim and hunt beneath Antarctic sea ice.

BASS ROCK
SCOTLAND, UK

Bass Rock in Scotland's Firth of Forth has the world's largest colony of breeding northern gannets. More than 75,000 pairs of birds breed on this tiny uninhabited island – around 60 percent of Europe's gannets. To catch fish, they circle high in the air, then nosedive into the sea at speeds of 60 mph (96 kph).

PENGUINS

The ocean is a good hunting ground for any bird that can catch fish – and penguins are among the most expert fishers of them all. These flightless birds of the southern hemisphere also prey on squid and krill, using flipper-like wings to propel themselves forward underwater. An emperor penguin can hold its breath for up to 20 minutes while diving for food!

SCOTLAND
BASS ROCK
IRELAND
UK
NORTH SEA
ATLANTIC OCEAN
EUROPE

COASTLINES, ROCKS, AND CLIFFS

Oceans are large bodies of water over solid rock foundations, surrounded by a rocky rim – the coastline. Whether an ocean's coastline is bare rock or covered by soft sand, this thin stretch of ground, where water meets land and tides ebb and flow, is a unique habitat for all kinds of wildlife.

Coastlines vary from sandy beaches to towering cliffs.

ROCKY SHORES

For most coastlines, a rocky shore marks where continental crust stretches down beneath the sea as continental shelf. Beyond this, the bottom of the ocean is made from heavier oceanic crust, and here volcanic eruptions push islands, such as Hawaii, to the surface – creating more rocky shores from solidified lava.

Water washes into cracks in the rock, gradually opening them up.

Small cracks get bigger, eventually forming caves.

A cave may break right through the headland, forming a natural arch.

WEATHERING AND EROSION

Rocks don't last forever. Even the hardest rock eventually breaks down into tiny particles. Wind, rain, waves, ice, and even living things like plant roots can break rock into smaller and smaller pieces through a process called weathering. These particles then get blown or washed away, and end up being scattered elsewhere, in a process called erosion.

Weathering breaks down rocks.

Erosion transports rock sediment downhill.

COASTAL CLIFFS

Cliffs usually form around coastlines with high, hard rocks that are less likely to erode, leading to steep, often dangerous, drops. But even cliffs can become unstable as wave action batters the rocks at the bottom, wearing away the base of the cliff so that entire sections higher up might crash down. Cliffs are popular habitats for seabirds that nest on ledges where they can't be reached, except by air.

A gannet and its baby nest on a cliff ledge.

HEADLANDS, CAVES, AND STACKS

Around the coastlines, waves crash against rocks again and again, causing them to gradually wear away. Soft rocks, like chalk, wear away faster, creating bays and caves. Harder rocks, like granite, last longer – sometimes forming headlands that jut out to sea, as the rock around the headland erodes more quickly. Even here, persistent waves can break through weaker areas, opening archways that eventually collapse to leave tall stacks and shorter stumps.

AUSTRALIA

THE TWELVE APOSTLES

THE TWELVE APOSTLES
AUSTRALIA

Along the coastline of Victoria, southern Australia, erosion of the soft limestone rock has left a series of dramatic stacks up to 164 ft. (50 m) high. They are called the Twelve Apostles, although there have never been more than eight, and one of these recently collapsed into the sea!

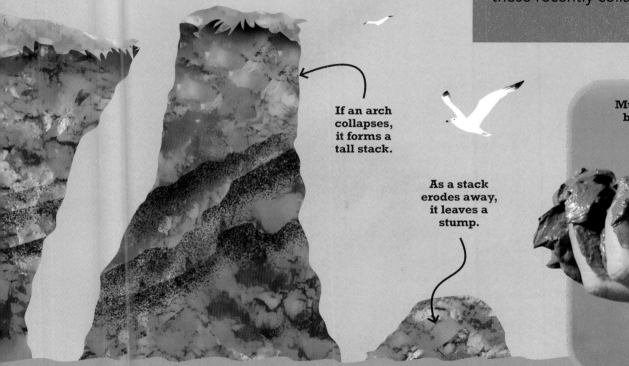

If an arch collapses, it forms a tall stack.

As a stack erodes away, it leaves a stump.

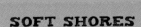

Mud is thick and squelchy because its particles all stick together.

ESTUARIES

An estuary is formed where a river flows into the sea. Estuaries often have banks either side made of long stretches of mud, which form when sediment is dropped from the river flow. Where rivers meet the sea, flowing freshwater dilutes the salty ocean, just as tides sometimes bring salty water a short distance upriver.

SOFT SHORES

Beaches and mudflats, called "soft shores," build up when sediments get deposited along coastlines. On beaches, the particles are grains of sand. These look small, but the particles that make up mud are even tinier – most are too small to see through a microscope! They cling together to make mud sticky, unlike sand, which can run through your fingers.

COASTAL ZONATION OF LIFE

In the short distance between the sea and the land, animals and seaweeds face an abrupt change in habitat – from an underwater world to an air-breathing world. Most living things stick to one or the other, either land or water, but what about those that live between the tides?

ZONATION OF LIFE

Between the sea and the shore, animals and seaweeds have adapted in different ways depending on how much time they spend in the air and underwater. As you move up the shore away from the sea, the habitat changes, and one community of living things replaces another. These different habitats are known as "zones," and the change of organisms between the zones is called zonation.

Only the hardiest creatures live around exposed shorelines.

LIVING UNDER THE WAVES

Some organisms cling onto rocky shores better than others, which helps them survive the battering waves and not get swept out to sea. Leafy seaweeds can be ripped apart fairly easily, so seaweed grows thickest on calm or sheltered shores. Where big waves bring water higher up the shore, communities of living things might shift closer to dry land.

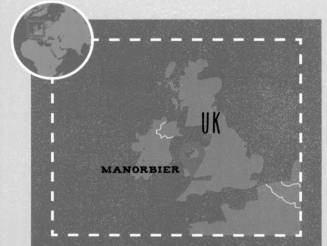

UK

MANORBIER

MANORBIER
WALES, UK

A wide rocky shore of Manorbier Bay in south Wales is home to an especially rich variety of creatures, including many interesting species of snails and seaweeds. As the third-largest marine Special Area of Conservation (SAC) in the UK, the bay is a protected area and features many different habitats, including estuaries, mud and sand flats, lagoons, and caves. The area is even home to gray seals.

LOWER SHORE LIFE

Organisms living on the lower shore are almost always covered by water, unless the tide is extremely low. These include slimy clumps of seaweeds called wracks (see page 54), as well as snails and crabs, none of which can survive long out of water.

LOWEST LOW TIDE

Lichens live on rocks on the upper shore.

UPPER SHORE LIFE
Organisms that live higher on the shore spend most of their time out of the water, unless spring tides bring water higher than usual. Here, there are lichens and periwinkles that survive for longer in the air. Between the lower and upper shore is the middle shore zone. Life here spends around 50 percent of its time underwater and 50 percent in air.

THE DOUBLE LIFE
At high tide, when they are covered by water, seaweeds can photosynthesize, snails can graze, and fish can swim. And all these creatures only breed underwater. But at low tide, most don't do much. Animals huddle into rocky crannies or hide from the Sun's rays under blankets of seaweed. Some might find shelter in water-filled tidal pools.

HIGHEST HIGH TIDE

LOWEST HIGH TIDE

Barnacles and mussels keep their shells tightly shut when the tide is out.

Acorn barnacles feed when the tide comes in.

TIDAL CHALLENGES
Many organisms in the middle of the shore, such as seaweeds, slow-moving sea snails, and barnacles, lead double lives because they are caught in a place that can be covered by water at high tide and exposed to air at low tide. Most of them come from the sea originally, so they become more active when the tide is high.

HIGHEST LOW TIDE

THE REACH OF THE TIDE
How far up the shore the tides reach changes depending on the position of the Moon and Sun (see pages 48–49). Tidal water is much higher on a spring tide than on a neap tide, so some species may only be underwater during spring tides.

Anemones live on the lower shore, where they are usually underwater.

TIDAL POOLS

A rocky shore does not just rise smoothly from the sea to the land. There are crags, dips, boulders, and crevices where rocks have been worn down and carved out by weathering. Tidal pools form in these dips and crevices as pockets of seawater are left behind after high tide. This is where many coastal organisms make their homes.

A MINIATURE SEAWATER HOME

Tidal pools provide a safe haven for seawater animals that might otherwise be left stranded at low tide. The tiniest pools of water can dry out completely in the Sun, but bigger ones stay full all the time. Some organisms even make the biggest tidal pools their permanent home.

Some starfish and anemones live their entire lives in one tidal pool.

Common prawns can be found in shallow tidal pools.

UNDERWATER SHELTER

Because tidal pools provide a watery shelter during low tides, they often contain animals or seaweeds that would usually live lower down the shore, under the water. Pools may contain red seaweeds, anemones, and shrimps that can continue feeding and swimming about, even when the tides recede and all around them the exposed shore is drying under the Sun.

GUARDING TERRITORIES

Some fish, such as the European shanny, stay put within their pool even when the tide rises above them. Their sheltered dip in the rock is still a good place for feeding and breeding when it is several feet under the sea. So rather than swimming out into the ocean, these fish guard their tidal pool homes and chase away any intruders that come too close.

A shanny stays put in its rock pool home.

CHANGING TEMPERATURES

The temperature inside tidal pools changes more quickly than in the vast expanse of the ocean. On a sunny day, tidal pools warm up, whereas in chilly weather they might get colder than the sea. And, just like changing salt levels (see below), the smaller the pool, the bigger the temperature change will be.

The epaulette shark has adapted to hold its breath and "walk" across rocky coastal terrain.

CANADA

BOTANICAL BEACH

USA

BOTANICAL BEACH
VANCOUVER, CANADA

The long stretch of flat sandstone and granite coastal rock on the western coast of Vancouver is famous for its colorful tidal pool wildlife – including purple starfishes, blue mussels, green anemones, and sea cucumbers.

Green seaweeds and algae release bubbles of oxygen as they photosynthesize.

OXYGEN LEVELS

Oxygen levels in a tidal pool change, too. Warmer water holds less oxygen than colder water, so in warm pools, oxygen levels might drop. But if these same pools contain seaweed, the seaweed might boost the oxygen levels with its photosynthesis. These changes affect virtually all living things because they all need oxygen to survive.

ADAPTING TO SALT

Tidal pools are often full of life, but the conditions within them can change dramatically, so living here isn't always easy. When the Sun shines, water evaporates but salt stays behind – which means the pool gets saltier. When it rains, pools get diluted with freshwater. The animals and seaweeds living inside tidal pools must be able to adapt to these changes to survive.

Water evaporates from the pool but salt remains.

INCREASED SALINITY (MORE SALTY)

Precipitation dilutes water in the pool.

DECREASED SALINITY (LESS SALTY)

SANDY BEACHES

A wide sandy beach is what many of us associate with the best kind of vacation – sand is comfortable to walk on barefoot and is the perfect spot for play and relaxation. But to plants and animals, a sandy beach can be a difficult and unpredictable place to live, and most choose not to live here at all!

THE NATURE OF SAND

A grain of sand is actually a tiny piece of sediment that is between 0.0025 in. and 0.079 in. (0.06 mm and 2 mm) in size. Most sand is made of broken down bits of rock, but shells of tiny marine animals also add color to the mix. Beaches are built by waves with a strong swash that drop more sediment than they wash away (see page 46). They gradually build up along the coast over time.

SHIFTING SANDS

Unlike mud, sand does not stick together – a sandcastle soon crumbles. This makes it a difficult place for plants to live because sand shifts around a lot over time, and very few plants can set root. Unlike rocky shores, seaweeds are missing from sandy beaches because they have nowhere to cling with their sucker-like holdfasts.

MATIRA BEACH
TAHITI

Among the whitest of tropical sand beaches, Matira Beach in Tahiti is made up of a chalky mineral (calcium carbonate), which comes from the hard skeletons of rocky corals in nearby reefs. The coral-grazing parrotfish (see opposite) that live there can poop up to 992 lb. (450 kg) of sand a year, and this goes toward making beautiful beaches like Matira.

TAHITI

PACIFIC OCEAN

NEW ZEALAND

ANIMALS ON THE SURFACE

Most bigger animals only visit sandy beaches occasionally, perhaps drawn by tasty scraps washed up from the sea. Some come just a few times a year to reproduce. Sand provides a perfect place for ocean turtles to lay their eggs (see page 76). Away from the reach of high tide, they bury their eggs, called a clutch, and leave them to incubate in the Sun's warmth.

Some kinds of male sand crabs are tiny – sometimes just 0.09 in. (2.5 mm) long!

LIVING BENEATH

Burrowing animals struggle on sandy beaches because sand isn't sturdy enough to hold its shape, so creatures cannot keep their burrows open. A few animals, such as sand crabs, choose to burrow through the sand, hiding from birds and other predators that might be prowling on the surface. Other microscopic creatures live between grains of sand, but most burrowing creatures prefer muddy shores.

Sun, sea, sand – and parrotfish poop!

WHITE BEACHES

In the tropics (the area of the Earth around the equator), white sand comes from the chalky skeletons of rocky coral, and some fish play a surprising part. Parrotfish have strong jaws to crunch up and eat coral – they spend around 90 percent of their day nibbling. The rocky bits pass through them and they poop it out as sand, which eventually washes up nearby to help form a beach. So the white sandy beaches that we relax on actually contain parrotfish poop!

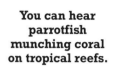

You can hear parrotfish munching coral on tropical reefs.

GOLDEN BEACHES

Many beaches around the world have golden-yellow sand. Under a magnifying glass, this sand consists of colorless, yellow, or brownish particles with the edges worn smooth. They are made from quartz – a mineral that is plentiful in Earth's rocks. Quartz is hard and does not easily react chemically with things around it, such as seawater. This makes it more likely to build up, to form beaches, and stay there.

BLACK BEACHES

A few beaches are black. The darker grains of sand contain different kinds of minerals because they are typically made from volcanic rock, such as basalt, which forms when lava hardens. This explains why black beaches usually form around the coasts of volcanic islands, such as Hawaii (see pages 116–117).

MUDFLATS

Mud can be squelchy, sticky, and sometimes very smelly, but for many living things it is the best place to make a home. Plants set root in it, animals burrow to safety under its surface – and many others find their food by foraging on the surface.

THE NATURE OF MUD

Mud is made up of particles of rock that are so tiny they can't even be seen through an ordinary microscope. These particles get mixed with detritus (natural waste from plants and animals) and slimy-coated microbes. The mixture is tightly packed together, producing something that sticks in clumps when it's wet.

Mudflats provide plenty of food for coastal creatures, such as crabs.

Shorebirds pluck worms and other invertebrates from the mud.

MUDFLATS

Particles of mud can be carried to the coast by rivers or washed ashore by the tide. Just like sand, mud particles are dropped by water and collect to form soft shores. Mud collects better in some places than others, such as on the banks around estuaries, where it can build up over great expanses to create mudflats. Because mud is thick and sticky, it doesn't shift around as easily as sandy beaches.

Cockles hide just below the surface of the mud.

Lugworms live in tunnels about 8 in. (20 cm) deep.

BURROWING IN MUD

Mud doesn't crumble as much as sand; it tends to keep its shape when animals burrow through it and so their burrows stay open. This means that mudflats usually contain many more burrowing animals than sand does, including worms and cockles. Most of these animals stay quite close to the surface rather than venturing down into the muddy depths.

FEEDING ON THE SURFACE

There are plenty of edible goodies for birds in the mud and they will sometimes arrive in their millions. Many shorebirds, such as sandpipers, flock to mudflats in winter to feed – a journey they make every year. Short-billed birds, like plovers, grab invertebrates near the surface, whereas birds with longer bills, such as godwits and curlews, reach deeper prey, including worms, shrimps, and crabs.

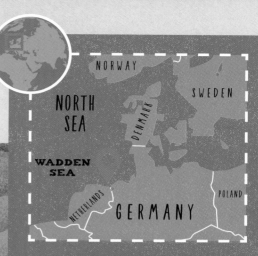

WADDEN SEA
NORTH SEA

A stretch of gently sloping coastline in northern Europe, called the Wadden Sea, has the world's largest system of sand and mudflats. This protected region is an important habitat for wildlife, and a stopover for many thousands of migratory birds that hunt for prey in the mud.

Each mound of sand marks a lugworm burrow.

CONDITIONS IN THE MUD

Whereas water drains easily through sand, it clings to mud, which tends to stay wet. This is good for keeping ocean animals wet but makes the circulation of fresh mud and oxygen difficult – so oxygen is quickly used up by mud-dwelling creatures. This explains why most animals, such as worms, stay near the surface, where they can breathe through their burrow openings.

Lugworms swallow mud and then poop it out at the surface.

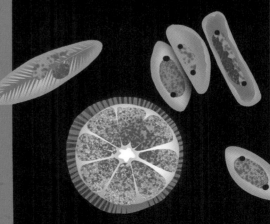

WHY IS MUD SMELLY?

An inch or so below the surface, where oxygen levels drop, mud often turns black. Black mud contains bacteria that survive without oxygen. These bacteria live using chemical processes that generate gases, which can give the mud a nasty smell.

Gases such as methane can make the mud smell like rotting eggs!

SALT MARSHES AND MANGROVES

Although oceans are home to many seaweeds, most true plants fail to thrive in ocean habitats; they cannot stand the salt and have difficulty rooting on rocky shores or sandy beaches. But in some muddy places where they can keep their leaves above the water surface, special types of plants have made their homes.

Salicornia is a salt-tolerant plant (halophyte) that thrives in salt marshes.

THE PROBLEM WITH SEAWATER

A typical land plant absorbs water through its roots, which gets drawn up through the stem to replace the water that evaporates from its leaves. But if the roots are surrounded by salt, this can actually draw water out of the plant, leaving it dehydrated. So, to survive near the sea, coastal plants need to stop this from happening.

DRAWING UP THE WATER

Plants that thrive in salty conditions are called halophytes, and many of them survive by collecting so much salt in their leaves that they become saltier than the seawater around their roots. This means that their leaves can pull water up through the stem and roots with more strength than surrounding seawater can draw it out.

Salt is left behind on the leaves of some halophytes.

FILTERING OUT THE SALT

The roots of halophytes also have a special filter that catches most of the salt that comes from the water. The filter wraps round the tiny pipes that carry water through the roots, so the nutrient-filled water rising through the stem, called sap, is much fresher than seawater. Some halophytes also have glands in their leaves that get rid of excess salt, leaving salty crystals on their surface.

SALT MARSHES

Types of halophytes living on the upper reaches of mudflats only get flooded at high tide. This is called a salt marsh. Just like on the rocky shore, there is often a different community of species on the upper shore compared with the lower shore, called zonation (see pages 84–85). Salt marsh grasses, such as cord grass, thrive in this habitat.

Salt marsh plants are the first to grow on coastal mudflats.

MANGROVES

Along stretches of muddy coastline in the tropics, salt-tolerant trees called mangroves make up a unique kind of habitat. Heavy trees need extra support in sloppy mud to avoid falling over. To get this support, many grow with their roots spread wide to form a large base. Some trees grow far-reaching shallow roots called "buttress roots" that help stop the tree from toppling over.

Mangroves grow in shallow, tropical lagoons.

ADAPTING TO MUD

Mangroves have remarkable ways of staying healthy in mud that has little oxygen. Some have air-breathing "stilt roots" that arch down from the trunk like spider's legs. Others have root tips that point up out of the mud, like a snorkel. And all mangroves contain a honeycomb-like system of chambers that help carry air down below the muddy surface.

Pointed mangrove roots take in oxygen from above the mud surface.

SUNDARBANS MANGROVE FOREST
SOUTH ASIA

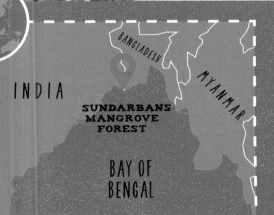

INDIA

BANGLADESH

MYANMAR

SUNDARBANS MANGROVE FOREST

BAY OF BENGAL

The Sundarbans is a coastal region in the Bay of Bengal that is the world's largest single area of mangrove forest. Covering 3,861 sq. mi. (10,000 sq km), the area is home to a large diversity of Asian wildlife, including regal Bengal tigers and Gangetic dolphins.

CONTINENTAL SHELVES AND SLOPES

Around the edges of the world's continents, shallow water sits above continental rock that stretches far out to sea. These are the continental shelves. Here, the water is usually no more than 656 ft. (200 m) deep, and contains some of the richest communities of life found anywhere in the ocean.

Shoals of fish find plenty to eat around coastlines.

COASTAL RICHNESS

Life is so rich in coastal seas because water running off the land and the movement of the currents bring an abundance of life-giving nutrients. Rivers flow into the sea, along with organic matter and minerals from rocks. Upwellings of ocean water rising toward the surface bring even more nutrients from deeper waters (see page 45).

Coastline

CONTINENTAL SHELF

COASTAL FOOD CHAINS

Microscopic algae swarm near the sunlit surface, feeding on particles of nutrients. These algae are the first step in the ocean food chains – without them, other creatures would have nothing to eat. Algae are eaten by tiny planktonic animals which, in turn, are eaten by fish (see page 42). Coastal seas are home to some of the biggest shoals of fish on the planet, and also where we source fish to eat.

Shallow coastal seas are home to many different species.

PERU
SOUTH AMERICA

The cold Humboldt current, flowing up the eastern coast of South America, brings upwellings of deep ocean water. These are so full of nutrients that huge shoals of fish gather here to feed. The fisheries around Peru account for 20 percent of the worldwide ocean catch!

SOUTH AMERICA

PERU

PACIFIC OCEAN

COASTAL DIVERSITY

The shallow seas above the continental shelf account for less than 10 percent of the world's ocean surface, yet they contain more than 90 percent of all known ocean wildlife!

CHANGING FORTUNES

The peak of the last ice age happened a quarter of a million years ago. During this time, shallow seas, such as those around Indonesia or between New Guinea and Australia, dried up – but you wouldn't guess it today. Even though these seas are quite young, life has bloomed fast, and they are home to an incredibly diverse range of creatures.

INDONESIA
NEW GUINEA
AUSTRALIA

The Sunda Shelf was once above sea level, but is now shallow seas and islands.

Giant kelp forests grow in nutrient-filled water.

Freshwater from land

UNDERWATER FORESTS

Corals, seaweeds, and a few kinds of plants are fixed to the sea bottom and grow underwater along the coasts – wherever they can bathe in the light of the Sun. In some places, plants and algae create rich underwater communities, and are sometimes called "the rainforests of the sea."

Carelessly thrown away plastic and waste pollute the oceans.

VULNERABLE SEAS

Being so close to the land can make coastal seas vulnerable as nutrients are not the only things that wash from the land into the sea. Man-made pollution in the form of chemical waste and trash end up in the water, too. Some coastal seas are among the most polluted parts of the ocean, harming sea life and destroying habitats.

CORAL REEFS

Coral reefs are the richest ocean habitats of all. They provide a sheltered area for many sea creatures to lay their eggs and are a safe place to feed and raise young. The reef is built out of corals with rocky skeletons, which provide homes for thousands of other species – including colorful clownfish, sea slugs, and roaming reef sharks.

WHAT IS A CORAL?

Corals are types of soft-bodied animals called cnidarians – a group that also includes jellyfish and anemones. The living flesh of a coral is actually a colony of thousands of tiny polyps, each with feeding tentacles. The colony builds its own skeleton for support. In soft corals, the skeletons are rubbery and flexible; in hard corals, the skeletons are like rock.

MANY SPECIES

Coral reefs are home to more than a quarter of all known ocean-dwelling species. Many of these species are specialized to do a unique job and compete very little with each other, as each job is essential to the ecosystem. Some species have special relationships that benefit both animals. The diet of a cleaner wrasse includes parasites that it cleans off other fish – the wrasse gets a meal and the fish stay clean and healthy.

FORMING A REEF

Over time, perhaps hundreds of years, a rocky colony grows so big that it becomes a dominant feature of the ocean – a reef. Most coral reefs grow best close to the surface, where water is warm and clear, and sunlight attracts the plankton that the coral eats.

Cleaner wrasse clean the teeth of other fish!

BIRTH OF A COLONY

A coral begins its life as a microscopic fertilized egg that grows into a single tiny polyp. The polyp builds itself a cup-shaped skeleton around its soft body to protect it. Coral polyps living together in a colony gradually form a reef made up of layers of hard, skeletal rock, which can stretch for thousands of miles.

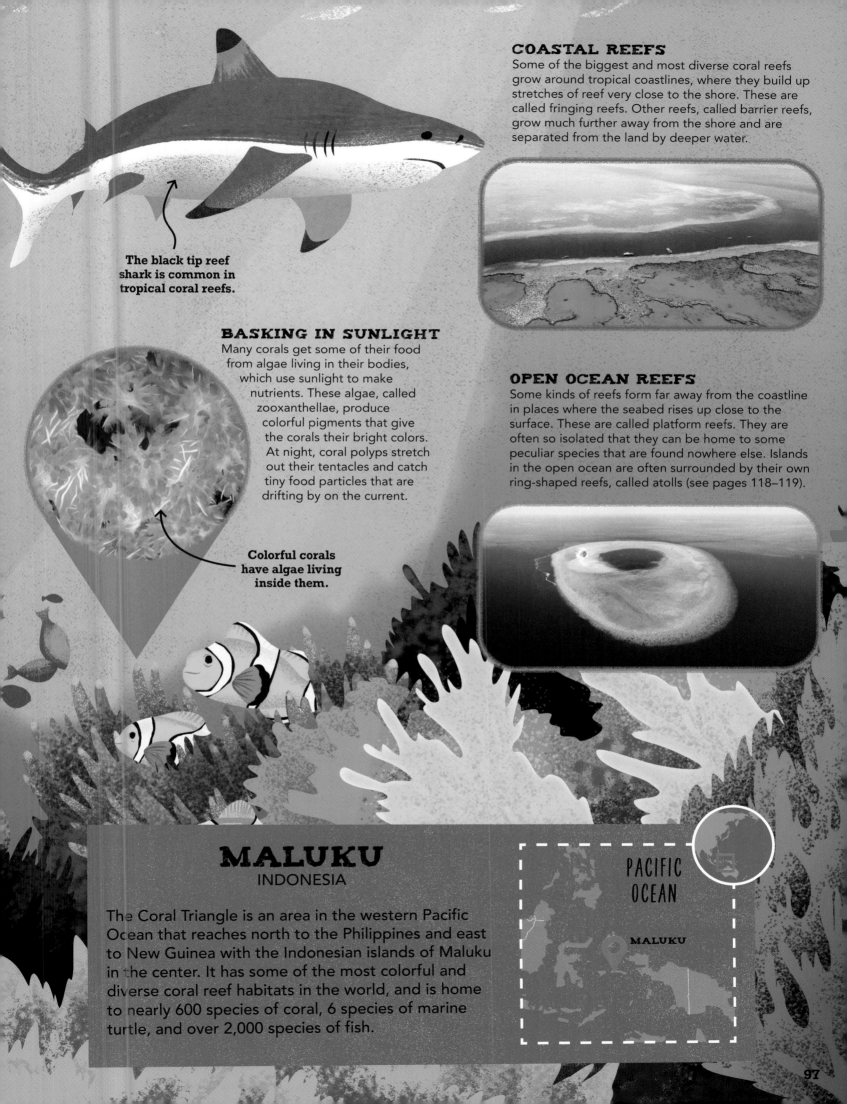

The black tip reef shark is common in tropical coral reefs.

COASTAL REEFS

Some of the biggest and most diverse coral reefs grow around tropical coastlines, where they build up stretches of reef very close to the shore. These are called fringing reefs. Other reefs, called barrier reefs, grow much further away from the shore and are separated from the land by deeper water.

BASKING IN SUNLIGHT

Many corals get some of their food from algae living in their bodies, which use sunlight to make nutrients. These algae, called zooxanthellae, produce colorful pigments that give the corals their bright colors. At night, coral polyps stretch out their tentacles and catch tiny food particles that are drifting by on the current.

Colorful corals have algae living inside them.

OPEN OCEAN REEFS

Some kinds of reefs form far away from the coastline in places where the seabed rises up close to the surface. These are called platform reefs. They are often so isolated that they can be home to some peculiar species that are found nowhere else. Islands in the open ocean are often surrounded by their own ring-shaped reefs, called atolls (see pages 118–119).

MALUKU
INDONESIA

The Coral Triangle is an area in the western Pacific Ocean that reaches north to the Philippines and east to New Guinea with the Indonesian islands of Maluku in the center. It has some of the most colorful and diverse coral reef habitats in the world, and is home to nearly 600 species of coral, 6 species of marine turtle, and over 2,000 species of fish.

PACIFIC OCEAN

MALUKU

OCEAN FORESTS AND MEADOWS

Coral reefs are habitats made by and of animals, but in other parts of the world, coastal seas are blanketed with seaweeds or plants, forming unique patches of underwater vegetation. Imagine vast forests and meadows, like the ones we have on land, but swaying in the underwater currents.

KELP FORESTS

Giant kelp is the world's biggest kind of seaweed. Its long leafy fronds can reach up to 148 ft. (45 m) from base to tip and can grow more than 1.6 ft. (0.5 m) each day, making it one of the fastest growing living things in the world. In the cool waters around the Pacific North American coast, where upwellings bring nutrients from the deep, kelp forms magnificent underwater forests.

The holdfast clings to a rocky base.

LIFE OF A GIANT SEAWEED

Like almost all seaweeds, giant kelp needs a rocky base on which to grow. It attaches itself to hard rock by a holdfast, rather than having roots (see page 54). Once it is secure, giant kelp grows rapidly toward sunlight. Even when its holdfast is in deep water, its fronds can reach the sunlit surface and stretch out to form a thick, leafy canopy.

LIFE IN THE KELP FOREST

Many invertebrates, such as sea urchins, rely on giant kelp for food. Other animals prey on the invertebrates living there and use the kelp for shelter – just like forest animals would do on land. Sharks, seals, and sea lions hunt for prey among the fronds and, in Pacific North America, sea otters dive below the kelp to collect shellfish from the bottom.

Sea otters hunt and play in giant kelp.

Carpets of seagrass form underwater meadows.

UNDERWATER MEADOWS

Although some specialized plants, such as mangroves and salt marsh grasses, manage to survive in salty water, only one kind of true plant succeeds permanently below the surface of the sea – down to a depth of about 33 ft. (10 m). These are seagrasses. In sunlit shallows around the world, they can spread out to form a unique ocean habitat: an underwater grassy meadow.

ADAPTING TO OCEAN LIFE

Seagrasses grow in sand and can tolerate salt in the water because they hold salt within them – this stops them from losing water and becoming dehydrated. The grassy, strap-like leaves are an important adaptation to coping with strong ocean currents; the currents easily flow around the leaf blades without uprooting the plant. Some seagrasses, such as eelgrass, grow pod-like structures containing seeds that can float, helping the plant to spread its seeds.

Leaves

Long pods

Eelgrass is a type of seagrass that grows its seeds in pods.

Roots

A dugong vacuums up eelgrass.

EELGRASS GRAZERS

Like giant kelp, eelgrass is an important food source for many kinds of vegetarian animals, both on land and under the sea. At low tide, geese graze on its shoots, while underwater animals as varied as green turtles and manatees rely on the plants as their main source of food. The dense cover it provides offers vulnerable animals, such as fish fry and seahorses, with shelter from predators.

IZEMBEK NATIONAL WILDLIFE REFUGE
ALASKA, USA

One of the largest eelgrass meadows in the world grows in a lagoon inside Alaska's Izembek National Wildlife Refuge. The eelgrass here is habitat for abundant wildlife, including – during spring and fall – the entire population of emperor geese, which stop to rest as they migrate between their southern wintering and Arctic breeding grounds.

USA

IZEMBEK
NATIONAL
WILDLIFE
REFUGE

LIVING IN THE OPEN OCEAN

The open ocean is the most expansive habitat on the planet. Beyond the continental shelves, offshore waters plunge down to an average depth of 13,000–20,000 ft. (4,000–6,000 m). The oceans contain just over 240 million cubic miles (1 billion cubic kilometers) of water, stretching vast distances that look the same in all directions for as far as the eye can see.

FUELING OCEAN LIFE

Out in the open ocean, plant life consists almost entirely of microscopic algae (phytoplankton), because large leafy plants and seaweeds have nowhere to anchor. In spring, when the days get longer and the Sun shines more, these algae rapidly increase in numbers – this is called an algae bloom. As the summer passes, algae numbers decline as they are eaten by microscopic animals (zooplankton). In the tropics, a wide range of algae can survive throughout the year because of the high levels of sunshine.

A giant algae bloom can turn the water green or red!

OPEN OCEAN GRAZERS

On land, leaf-eating herbivores, such as elephants, are among the largest walking animals, but in the oceans, algae-grazers, such as krill, are very small. Here, they account for up to 80 percent of the zooplankton (see page 42) and provide food for many bigger animals in the open ocean.

SURVIVING IN OPEN WATER

Creatures living in the open ocean are surrounded by water on all sides, with nothing to provide shelter except, deeper down, the cover of darkness. Where the light does reach, animals are vulnerable to predators and need ways to avoid being seen, while predators also need cunning ways to hunt their prey.

Dolphinfish have shiny blue-green backs that blend in to the ocean environment.

Some fish have "gill rakers" inside their mouths to help trap prey.

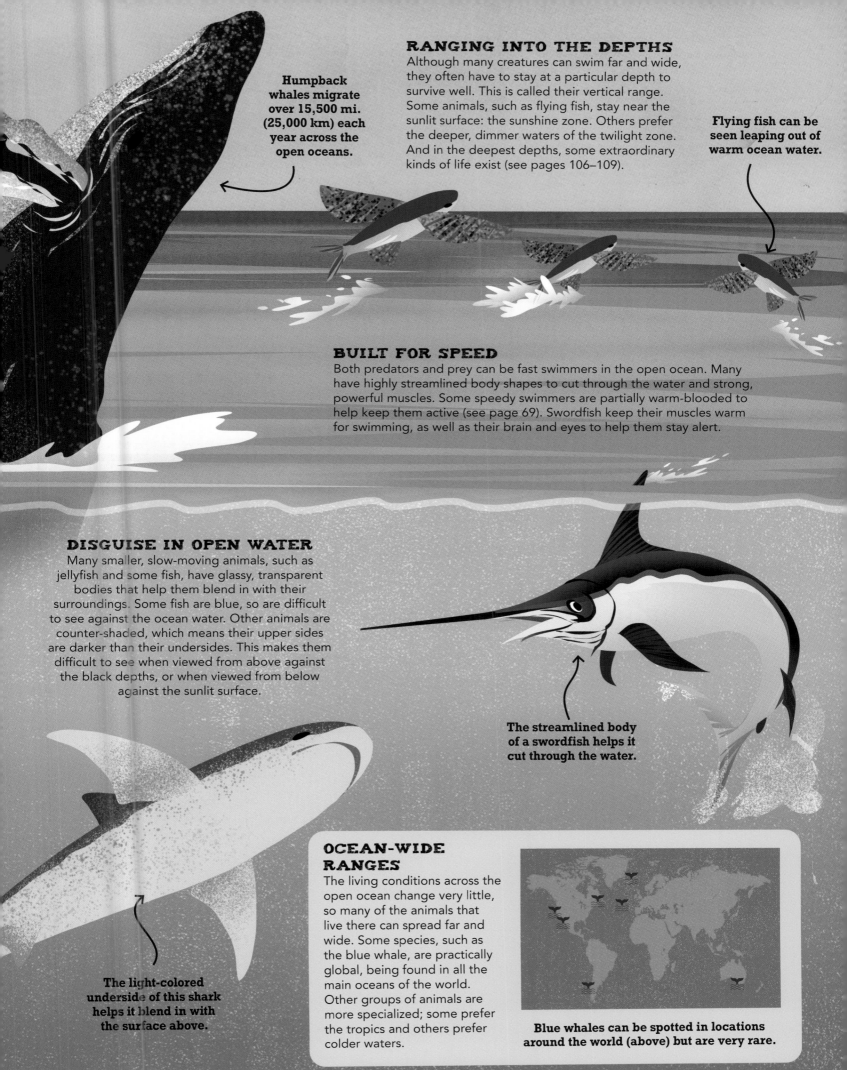

Humpback whales migrate over 15,500 mi. (25,000 km) each year across the open oceans.

RANGING INTO THE DEPTHS

Although many creatures can swim far and wide, they often have to stay at a particular depth to survive well. This is called their vertical range. Some animals, such as flying fish, stay near the sunlit surface: the sunshine zone. Others prefer the deeper, dimmer waters of the twilight zone. And in the deepest depths, some extraordinary kinds of life exist (see pages 106–109).

Flying fish can be seen leaping out of warm ocean water.

BUILT FOR SPEED

Both predators and prey can be fast swimmers in the open ocean. Many have highly streamlined body shapes to cut through the water and strong, powerful muscles. Some speedy swimmers are partially warm-blooded to help keep them active (see page 69). Swordfish keep their muscles warm for swimming, as well as their brain and eyes to help them stay alert.

DISGUISE IN OPEN WATER

Many smaller, slow-moving animals, such as jellyfish and some fish, have glassy, transparent bodies that help them blend in with their surroundings. Some fish are blue, so are difficult to see against the ocean water. Other animals are counter-shaded, which means their upper sides are darker than their undersides. This makes them difficult to see when viewed from above against the black depths, or when viewed from below against the sunlit surface.

The streamlined body of a swordfish helps it cut through the water.

The light-colored underside of this shark helps it blend in with the surface above.

OCEAN-WIDE RANGES

The living conditions across the open ocean change very little, so many of the animals that live there can spread far and wide. Some species, such as the blue whale, are practically global, being found in all the main oceans of the world. Other groups of animals are more specialized; some prefer the tropics and others prefer colder waters.

Blue whales can be spotted in locations around the world (above) but are very rare.

OCEAN MIGRATIONS

Some of the most impressive animal migrations on Earth happen across the world's seas. Whales cross entire oceans, and some seabirds span the whole planet. In each case, a powerful instinct, to reproduce or to feed, drives these animals to undertake their epic journeys.

WHAT ARE MIGRATIONS?

Migrations are when animals make periodic journeys from one place to another, often traveling great distances to find the best conditions for breeding or feeding. Migrations are usually round-trips, meaning the animals travel there and back again, and can occur because the animals need to be in different places at different times of year.

MIGRATIONS FOR OCEAN ANIMALS

Ocean animals migrate in different ways. Some move horizontally through the ocean, either between the equator and poles, or between the open ocean and the shoreline – and repeat this every year. Others move vertically through the water, migrating between different depths, on a daily basis.

Whales migrate horizontally, crossing entire oceans.

LONG-DISTANCE MIGRATIONS

Animals may undertake annual migrations across long stretches of ocean to take advantage of seasonal blooms of food. Many species of whales breed in the warmer waters near the tropics because, as warm-blooded creatures, young whales thrive better in the warmth. They then migrate toward the poles, where nutrient-filled colder waters support the vast quantities of plankton that can satisfy their enormous appetites.

POLE-TO-POLE

The longest migrations of all go almost pole-to-pole. After breeding in the Arctic summer, Arctic terns fly across coastal seas and reach Antarctica by November – a time that coincides with the southern summer. By enjoying both polar summers – when the Sun never sets (see pages 120–121) – at different ends of the world, they probably experience more sunshine than any other animal on the planet.

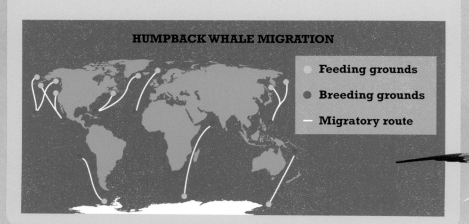

HUMPBACK WHALE MIGRATION

- Feeding grounds
- Breeding grounds
- Migratory route

Southbound migration →

Northbound migration →

MIGRATING INSHORE

Some animals migrate toward the shore to breed. Turtles must haul themselves onto beaches to lay their eggs, and many species of ocean fish move into shallower coastal water to spawn. Here, their eggs and young will find better shelter among seaweeds, reefs, or mangrove roots. Some fish, such as salmon, even migrate from the saltwater into freshwater rivers to spawn. Other fish, like freshwater eels, migrate in the opposite direction, and breed in the open sea.

Sockeye salmon swim from the sea to freshwater rivers.

Arctic summer breeding ground

Pit stop for feeding

Antarctic summer wintering ground

NINGALOO REEF

AUSTRALIA

NINGALOO REEF
AUSTRALIA

The migratory movements of some of the biggest animals on the planet are determined by food. Filter-feeding whale sharks, the biggest of all fish, migrate annually to Ningaloo Reef in western Australia, where they arrive to feed on krill and plankton that are drawn to the reef by spawning coral. The arrival of whale sharks is so predictable that Ningaloo has become a favorite location for biologists to study the world's biggest fish.

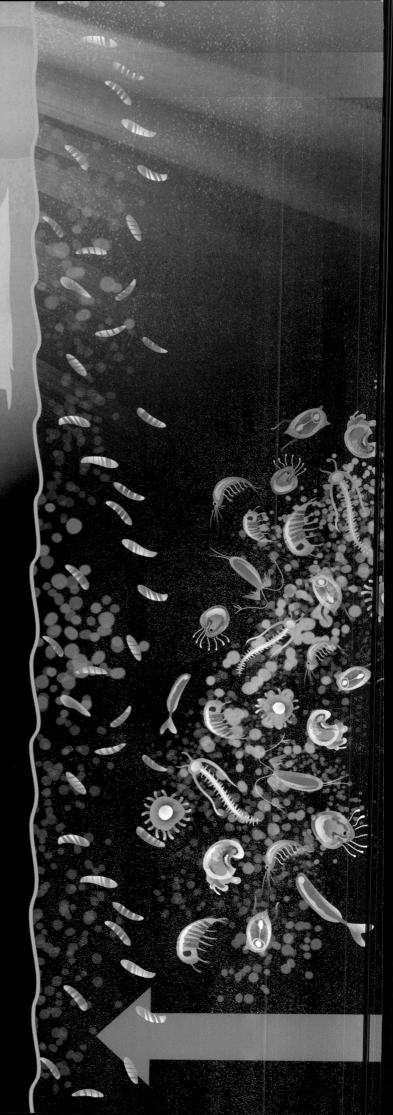

VERTICAL MIGRATION

One of the most remarkable migrations of all is one that is scarcely noticed. Each night, trillions of tiny planktonic animals rise upward in the water to feed on microscopic algae near the surface – then return to the ocean depths by day. They may be tiny, but when you weigh them all together, their movement ranks as the biggest migration on the planet.

RISING PLANKTON

Unlike most horizontal migrations, the rising plankton migration is actually made up of a mixture of hundreds of different species. These microscopic oceanic animals include tiny crustaceans called copepods, as well as larvae of crabs, fish, and other animals – all rising and falling according to the daily cycle. These kinds of 24-hour movements are called diel migrations, after the Latin word "dies," meaning "day."

WHAT IS THE CUE?

The drop in light levels is the most likely trigger that makes animals rise up to the surface at night – and this seems to play an important role. Even a solar eclipse can trigger the same movement from these creatures! Many animals also rely on their built-in body clocks to help them sense the 24-hour cycle.

BENEFITS OF A VERTICAL MIGRATION

It is thought that planktonic animals migrate in this way to avoid predators, because they are less likely to be seen under the cover of night. These tiny animals feed on phytoplankton (microscopic algae) that live near the surface (see pages 52–53), but they only rise up to do so when it's dark, returning to rest in safer, deeper waters by day.

CHAIN REACTION

Because planktonic animals are, themselves, food for bigger creatures, it is unsurprising that some bigger creatures follow the diel migration, too – in search of food. The knock-on effect with the food chain means that many other animals, such as fish, squid, and even filter-feeding sharks, rise toward the surface at night, too.

AN UNEXPECTED DISCOVERY

Ocean diel migration was not discovered by biologists, as you might expect, but by the US Navy. During World War II, sonar – a type of navigation technology – detected that something big and mysterious was rising and falling in the ocean. Marine biologists later confirmed that this was caused by billions of migrating planktonic animals.

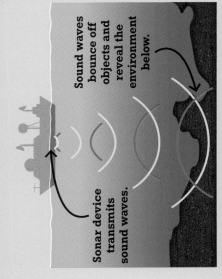

Sonar device transmits sound waves.

Sound waves bounce off objects and reveal the environment below.

VAADHOO ISLAND
MALDIVES, INDIAN OCEAN

INDIA

SRI LANKA

VAADHOO ISLAND

INDIAN OCEAN

Each night, around the shorelines of Vaadhoo Island, the surface of the sea sparkles with twinkly electric-blue lights – a phenomenon called the "sea of stars." The effect comes from light-making microbes that light up when disturbed by moving water. They are part of the vertical migration of plankton rising up to the surface at night.

THE DEEP SEA

Most of the open ocean habitat is dark and cold – at over 3,280 ft. (1,000 m) deep, it's too deep for light to reach. As the depth increases, the communities of animals change gradually, too. The species that live at the very bottom take on all sorts of weird and wonderful forms, and are like nothing else in the ocean – or indeed, the whole world.

THE CHALLENGES OF THE DEEP

Animals living in the deep ocean face four main problems: 1) it is too dark to see; 2) it is permanently cold; 3) the pressure is high enough to crush a car; and 4) food is very scarce. It might not be easy living, but these animals have evolved some of the most extraordinary adaptations to cope with the extreme conditions.

Also known as a spookfish, *Rhinochimaera* was discovered 5,310 ft. (1,620 m) deep!

A deep-sea brittle star.

Bioluminescent jellyfish live in the deep sea.

SENSING THE SURROUNDINGS

Many deep-sea animals have no eyes, so how do they get around? Anemones, sea cucumbers, and brittle stars at the bottom of the ocean are completely blind. They must rely on other senses – taste or touch – to find food. In the twilight zone, where rays of sunshine can just reach, some animals have enormous eyes to collect the faint light.

MAKING LIGHT

Where the Sun's light is very dim, or cannot reach at all, some animals can generate their own light in the darkness – a process called bioluminescence. This is enabled by special organs that contain light-producing bacteria. Some animals use their lights to attract prey or confuse predators; others are illuminated to attract mates.

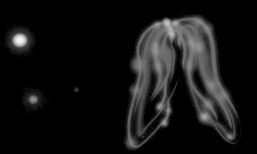

A REMOTE HABITAT

The ocean bottom is the least understood habitat for life on Earth. Its remoteness and very high pressure make it difficult to explore and study. The flat ocean bottom, called the abyssal plain, which is 19,685–26,247 ft. (6,000–8,000 m) down, makes up more than 50 percent of the Earth's seabed, yet most of it has never been explored by humans.

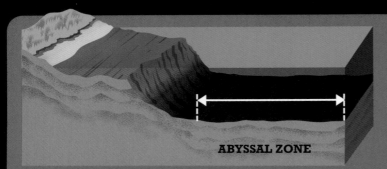

ABYSSAL ZONE

CAPE HATTERAS
NORTH CAROLINA, USA

Air-breathing animals usually stay close to the ocean surface, but some whales dive right down into the deep to find prey. Off Cape Hatteras -- a strip of land that stretches out into the Atlantic – Cuvier's beaked whales are the champions, diving deeper and longer than any other mammal, down to nearly 1.8 mi. (3 km).

USA

CAPE HATTERAS

ATLANTIC OCEAN

GETTING A MEAL

Living in such an extreme part of the ocean has its challenges, particularly when it comes to finding food. Many creatures living here will eat whatever they can find – usually waste matter and dead material that sinks down from above. These scavenging animals then get eaten by meat-eaters in turn.

Anglerfish have luminous lures to attract prey.

HUNTING IN THE DEEP

There can be so few animals swimming in the deep that hunters need special strategies to help them find prey. Many predatory fish have enormous mouths, large teeth, and expandable stomachs, so that they can swallow large prey that will keep them going for longer. Others, such as deep-sea anglerfish, entice prey with light-producing lures, and then gobble up the unsuspecting animal!

Cusk eels are among the deepest living fish.

SURVIVING THE COLD AND PRESSURE

All animals in the deepest part of the ocean are cold-blooded – their body temperature matches that of the surroundings. The cold keeps them sluggish most of the time, which means they do not need much food for fuel. Many animals save their energy for when they really need it – like on a hunt. Then, they spring into action with short bursts of speed.

THE OCEAN BOTTOM

Animals living on the abyssal plain at the ocean bottom are isolated from the normal cycle of night and day, and live in what can look like a peculiar, alien world. In fact, almost all of these animals have relatives found in shallower waters, but the deep-sea species are so specialized to their environment that they are unable to survive anywhere else.

CALM IN THE DEEP

Far away from the windblown waves at the surface, the current can hardly be felt at all just above the ocean floor. This means that as well as being cold and dark, the water is calm and for long periods of time little disturbs the sediment, except for the occasional movement of a few slow-moving animals.

WHO LIVES HERE?

Despite the bleak conditions, all kinds of diverse animals can be found on the ocean bottom. These include deep-sea shrimps, crabs, squat lobsters, octopuses, and spindly-legged sea spiders (unrelated to true spiders on land). In places, sea cucumbers are especially abundant – they gather in "herds" and bulldoze through the sediment in search of food.

Some sea cucumbers have pointy "sails."

GETTING FOOD

In shallower waters, where currents flow, filter-feeding animals rely on the movement of water to bring them nutrients. Down here on the ocean floor, there are no strong currents to rely on. Instead, most animals are deposit-feeders – they root around in the sediment at the sea bottom, which contains the dead and waste matter that constantly falls from living things swimming above.

This deep-sea octopus feeds near the ocean floor.

Deep-sea tube worms root in the seabed.

Sea pigs, a kind of sea cucumber, have chunky legs that help them crawl across the mud.

Sea cucumbers gather in "herds."

Giant isopods live in cold, deep waters.

UNDERWATER STORMS AND AVALANCHES

It may be calm a lot of the time down here, but the deep sea also experiences violent natural events. At times, cold water currents race across the ocean floor as part of the global system of ocean currents (see pages 44–45), creating underwater storms. And around the continental slope, where the abyssal plain rises up to meet the continental shelf, earthquakes may cause an avalanche of sediment to shake downward, smothering everything in its wake under a mudslide.

FISH OF THE OCEAN FLOOR

Deep-sea relatives of cod, called rattails (because of the shape of their tails), are among the most common kinds of fish found on the ocean bottom. Like some other fish of the deep sea, they produce eggs that float to the surface to hatch, where young rattails will find more nutrients. As they get older, they move down into greater depths.

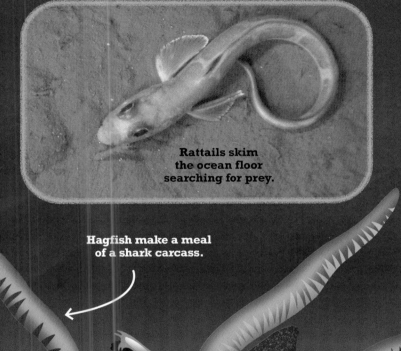

Rattails skim the ocean floor searching for prey.

Hagfish make a meal of a shark carcass.

ATLANTIC OCEAN

IRELAND   UK

PORCUPINE ABYSSAL PLAIN

EUROPE

PORCUPINE ABYSSAL PLAIN
ATLANTIC OCEAN

The Porcupine Abyssal Plain, plunging down to more than 13,120 ft. (4,000 m) on the floor of the northeast Atlantic, is one of the best-studied deep-water habitats – thanks to a floating scientific observatory that was set up in 2002. Sea cucumbers make up 90 percent of the animals spotted on the plain. There can be thousands of individuals per acre!

FEASTING IN THE DARK

Occasionally, something falls to the ocean bottom that brings a real feast. When large mammals die, such as whales and seals, their bodies sink to the bottom, where they provide food for many creatures. They are quickly covered in huge numbers of amphipods, a kind of shrimp, and other scavengers, such as hagfish. As cunning scavengers, hagfish use their eel-like bodies to burrow into carcasses, then rip away mouthfuls of flesh.

Brittle stars have long, flexible arms.

Feather stars catch particles of food with their feathery arms.

Sixgill sharks can smell meat from up to 0.25 mi. (0.4 km) away.

FOOD WITH DANGER

A whale carcass offers a rare chance to gorge. It might be weeks or even months before many animals get a similar meal. But every scavenger that visits runs the risk of becoming hunted themselves, because the scent of the meat also attracts bigger meat-eaters, such as deep-water sharks.

OCEAN FLOOR HOT SPOTS

In some areas of the deep ocean, volcanic heat from beneath the ocean floor spreads upward, heating jets of seawater, which then gush from vents at the bottom of the ocean. These jets are rich in minerals that are used by special kinds of bacteria, which – in turn – support food chains of animals that look and behave unlike anything else on Earth.

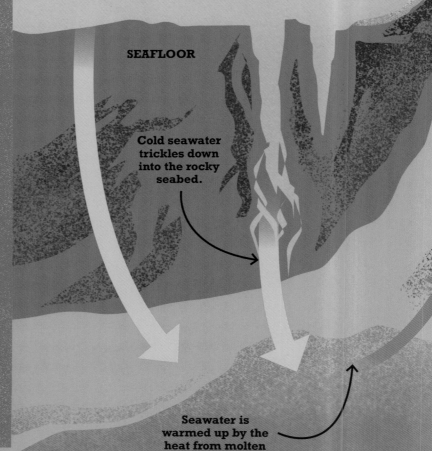

Dark cloud of hot, mineral-rich water

HEAT FROM UNDER THE ROCKS

Some regions of the ocean floor are volcanically active. In these areas, molten rock spews out of the Earth's crust, boiling the seawater as the flowing rock emerges from cracks in the ocean floor, before turning solid. This happens where the ocean floor is spreading apart (see pages 20–21), such as along the Mid-Atlantic Ridge and in the southeastern Pacific.

HYDROTHERMAL VENTS

All over the ocean floor, seawater continually trickles down through the rocks. But around the volcanic zones, these rocks were once molten and can stay hot for many years. This heats the seawater within the rock, forcing it upward through weaknesses in the ocean floor called hydrothermal vents. The erupting water is rich in minerals that have been concentrated by the high temperatures and pressures.

ATLANTIC OCEAN

AFRICA

MID-ATLANTIC RIDGE

SOUTH AMERICA

SEAFLOOR

Cold seawater trickles down into the rocky seabed.

MID-ATLANTIC RIDGE

ATLANTIC OCEAN

A curved line running the length of the Atlantic Ocean, from north to south, marks the position of the Mid-Atlantic Ridge. This is the boundary between two tectonic plates, and as new rock erupts from between them, the plates grow and push America and Africa further apart. Along the ridge, communities of animals, fueled by chemosynthetic bacteria, are abundant.

Seawater is warmed up by the heat from molten rocks deep down.

UNDERWATER CHIMNEYS

As hot seawater spews from a hydrothermal vent, it mixes with the cold water of the deep ocean. This makes the dissolved minerals solidify, and they build up over time into structures that look like chimneys. Many of these chimneys churn out black clouds of minerals called sulphides – so have been called "black smokers."

Tube worms live in darkness near vents on the ocean floor.

Thick mats of bacteria grow near warm jets of seawater.

FOOD FROM MINERALS

Slimy mats of bacteria grow on the walls of these chimneys. These special kinds of bacteria extract the minerals and use them in chemical reactions to generate energy. They use this energy to make their food from carbon dioxide. Unlike plants on land, this deep-sea food-generating process, called chemosynthesis, takes place in complete darkness, making it unique.

UNIQUE FOOD CHAINS

The food-making bacteria around hydrothermal vents support seafloor food chains that are the only ones on Earth living entirely independently of the Sun's energy. Some animals, such as shrimps, graze on the bacteria, and these are eaten by bigger predators, such as crabs and some fish.

HYDROTHERMAL VENT

A colony of hydrothermal mussels living on the slope of a vent.

Hot water and dissolved minerals

USING THE BACTERIA

Many animals that live around hydrothermal vents work together with the food-making bacteria, forming a "partnership." Tube worms and mussels have these bacteria living inside their bodies. The bacteria supply them with food, while the animal provides a safe home for the bacteria. This arrangement is very successful – tube worms and mussels often grow into huge colonies around the vents.

HOT BASALT ROCK

OCEAN TRENCHES

The very deepest parts of the ocean are great chasms in the rock that are carved out by movements of the Earth's crust, resulting in trenches that plunge even deeper than the abyssal plain – down to 36,000 ft. (11,000 m) below the ocean surface.

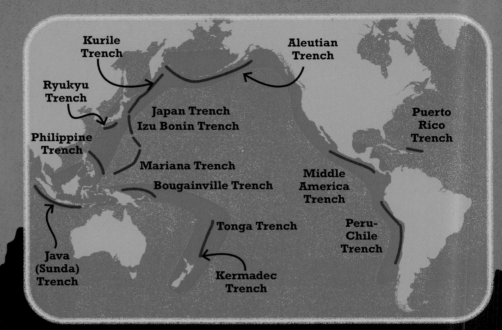

"Ring of Fire": areas prone to earthquakes and volcanic eruptions

Ocean trenches

Kurile Trench

Aleutian Trench

Ryukyu Trench

Japan Trench
Izu Bonin Trench

Puerto Rico Trench

Philippine Trench

Mariana Trench
Bougainville Trench

Middle America Trench

Peru-Chile Trench

Tonga Trench

Java (Sunda) Trench

Kermadec Trench

WHERE ARE THE TRENCHES?
The oceans of the world contain a total of 37 deep trenches, and 28 of these occur around the Pacific. They mark the Pacific "Ring of Fire" – an area around the biggest ocean where there are frequent earthquakes and volcanic eruptions because of tectonic plates moving around (see pages 20–21).

DIGGING THE TRENCH
The tectonic plates that make up the jigsaw of Earth's crust are always on the move – sometimes with dramatic effects. Violent collisions can happen between plates that are next to each other, particularly around the rim of the Pacific. Ocean trenches form when one plate dives beneath another, dragging the ocean floor down into a deep, dark chasm.

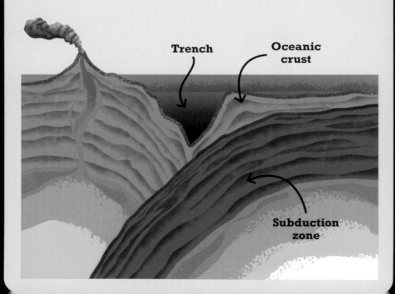

Trench

Oceanic crust

Subduction zone

THE DEEPEST TRENCH
The Mariana Trench in the western Pacific is the deepest trench in the world, making it the deepest known spot in the ocean. Here, the Pacific Plate, one that forms the biggest part of the Pacific floor, is moving slowly westward and plunging beneath the much smaller Mariana Plate. The trench plunges 36,000 ft. (11,000 m) down – further than the distance to the top of Mount Everest.

36,000 FT. (11,000 M)

ATACAMA TRENCH
SOUTH-EASTERN PACIFIC

In the southeastern Pacific, the oceanic Nazca Plate dives beneath South America to create the Atacama Trench (also known as the Peru-Chile Trench), which is 3,666 mi. (5,900 km) long and reaches a depth of 26,460 ft. (8,065 m). In 1960, this region of subduction was responsible for the largest earthquake ever recorded – in the neighboring region of Valdivia in Chile. It caused a tsunami, with waves up to 82 ft. (25 m) high, that reached as far as Hawaii, Australia, New Zealand, and the Philippines.

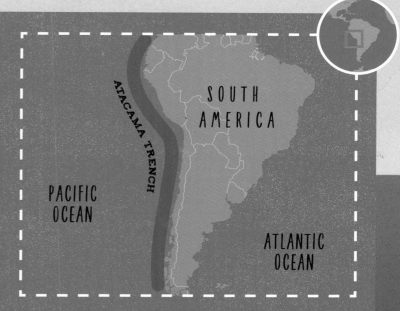

THE CHALLENGES OF A TRENCH

The deepest part of an ocean trench can be twice the depth of the abyssal plain on the ocean floor. Anything living here must not only survive double the pressure, it must also withstand unexpected and often violent natural events. Plunging plates cause underwater earthquakes, falling rocks, and crumbling sediment, but amazingly, even here some creatures make their homes.

Deep-sea snails have strong shells to withstand high pressure.

Red sea lilies have stalks that attach to the sea bottom.

Some jellyfish live at depths of 30,000 ft. (9,000 m).

MARIANA TRENCH

The free-swimming sea cucumber is also dubbed the "headless chicken fish."

OCEAN TRENCH COMMUNITIES

Trench-living animals are mostly versions of those living on the abyssal plain, but sea cucumbers are especially common here, making up 98 percent of the trench community. Most other animals are deposit-feeding worms and shrimps. Trench communities are more isolated from the surrounding ocean than the abyssal plain habitat, so some species here are unique to this extreme environment.

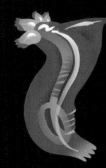

THE WORLD'S DEEPEST FISH

Few fish venture as deep as the ocean trenches, but there are some that take the plunge. Snailfish have soft, flabby bodies to help them tolerate the pressure, and are shaped like giant tadpoles. One species of snailfish was found 26,568 ft. (8,098 m) down in the Mariana Trench, which makes it the deepest-living fish so far recorded.

Snailfish are soft and translucent.

ISLAND DIVERSITY

Islands are areas of rock and sediment that rise up from the seabed and poke out above the water surface. Some islands are so big that they are more like miniature continents, but others are little more than specks in the wide ocean.

CONTINENTAL FRAGMENTS

The biggest islands, such as Madagascar and New Zealand, are continental fragments that are separated from their nearest landmasses by expanses of deep ocean. These fragments were created when tectonic plates moved slowly over millions of years, splitting continents, or making them collide (see pages 20–21). In some places, such as the Seychelles, only tiny continental fragments were created.

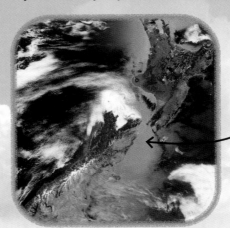

A continental fragment (New Zealand) slopes into deep water.

There are over 17,500 islands that make up the country of Indonesia, but some are very small!

Parrotfish live in shallow seas, munching on their favorite food – coral!

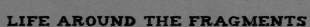

UNDERWATER CONTINENTS

The two main islands of New Zealand (North Island and South Island) are part of a massive continental shelf in the southwest Pacific that covers 1.9 million sq. mi. (5 million sq km). The land above water (New Zealand) makes up just 6 percent of the total size of the shelf. It is sometimes regarded as the Earth's eighth continent, called Zealandia, and provides habitats for many ocean animals found nowhere else.

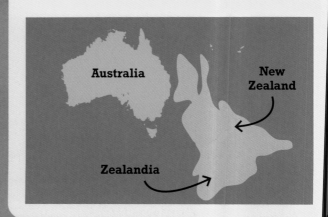

Australia

New Zealand

Zealandia

LIFE AROUND THE FRAGMENTS

These continental islands, such as the Seychelles, are surrounded by shelves – just like the main continents. In some places, these continental shelves are so expansive that they stretch out further than the island's land above the surface. The shallow water and sunlight make it the perfect place for a diverse range of creatures to live.

MARGINAL ISLANDS

Other large islands lie on shelves that are still connected to the main continental landmasses. In this way, Sumatra, Borneo, and Java are connected to Southeast Asia, and New Guinea is connected to Australia. It means that the oceans between them are never much more than 656 ft. (200 m) deep.

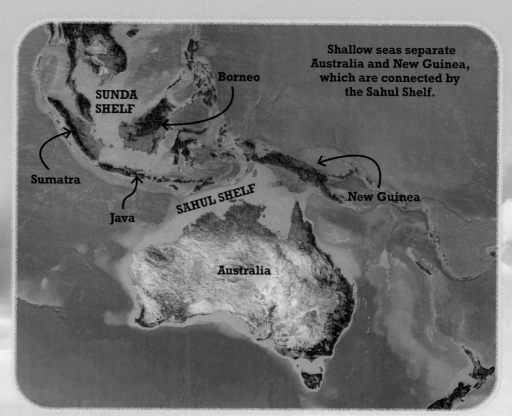

Shallow seas separate Australia and New Guinea, which are connected by the Sahul Shelf.

SUNDA SHELF

Borneo

Sumatra

Java

SAHUL SHELF

New Guinea

Australia

COMORO ISLANDS
INDIAN OCEAN

The Comoro Islands are a group of volcanic islands off the coast of Madagascar that are home to rare fish called coelacanths. These strange, secretive fish were discovered hiding in deep underwater caves around the base of the islands. Scientists believe that coelacanths are related to animals that lived hundreds of millions of years ago – but were thought to be extinct!

ISLANDS IN THE DEEP OCEAN

The smallest and most isolated islands are those that rise up from the deep ocean beyond the reach of the continental shelves – like Hawaii. These are formed from underwater volcanoes on the ocean floor that erupt to the surface, creating entirely new specks of land. Because these ocean islands are cut off from other land, they offer unique habitats for special types of organisms.

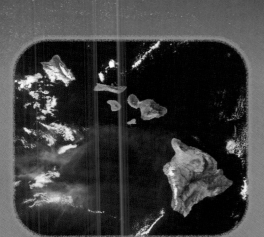

The Hawaiian islands are about 1,860 mi. (3,000 km) away from land.

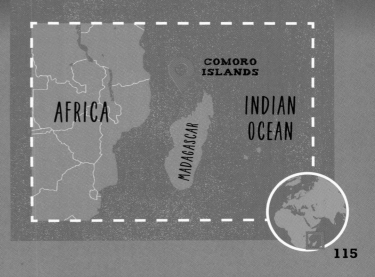

COMORO ISLANDS

AFRICA

INDIAN OCEAN

MADAGASCAR

OCEANIC ISLANDS

Islands that emerge from the deep ocean are not only small and remote, they are also places where life has evolved in its own way, away from species that exist elsewhere. When such an island is first created, its land and coasts begin barren and lifeless. This provides fresh opportunities for any creatures that discover the new land, as there is less competition for food and space.

MOUNTAIN GIANTS

Believe it or not, Mount Everest isn't actually the tallest mountain in the world – measured from the ocean floor, some underwater mountains are even taller! Mauna Kea in Hawaii stretches up to over 32,800 ft. (10,000 m) from base to peak, but more than half of it is hidden underwater. Only 13,120 ft. (4,000 m) is above sea level!

The Hawaiian islands are part of an arc formed by a series of hot-spot volcanoes.

Red-hot molten rock cools and solidifies.

NEW LIFE

After they erupt from the Earth's crust, all volcanic islands begin as hot, barren rock that are empty of life – both above and below the water. As they cool, animals begin to colonize. Seeds reach the land, blown on air or carried by water, and bring new plant life. Other ocean animals reach new islands by swimming or drifting on currents.

SUCCESSION

Over time, the exposed rock begins to weather and erode, creating sediment and soil, which helps plants to take root on land. Similarly, corals and seaweeds can grow around the rim of the island, and the coastal seas become increasingly nourished by nutrients from the land. As more and more organisms colonize the island, the first animals to have arrived are joined or replaced by species that arrive later. This changing mix of creatures is called "ecological succession," as species are "succeeded," or followed, by new ones.

Galápagos sharks were first identified around the Galápagos Islands.

EVOLUTION IN ISOLATION

Oceanic islands can last for millions of years. During this time, the organisms that have colonized the island may evolve into unique species that develop depending on their environment. For instance, on the Galápagos Islands, the marine iguana has evolved to be the only lizard in the world to graze on seaweed under the ocean. This is especially common on the most isolated islands – where new arrivals are less likely to breed with animals from neighboring areas.

NEW LAND FROM BENEATH THE WAVES

Volcanic islands rise from the Earth's crust in places where heat from inside the planet melts rock, and this molten lava spews to the surface through gaps and weaknesses. The lava then cools and solidifies to form layers of hard volcanic rock. Violent eruptions from the ocean bottom can pile rock up and up until it reaches the surface – and an island is formed.

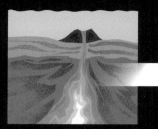

1. A volcano erupts on the seabed, pushing molten rock above the ocean crust.

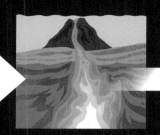

2. As the molten rock piles up and solidifies in layers, it forms a cone-shaped mound.

3. When the volcano emerges above the water's surface, an island is created.

VOLCANIC OCEAN FLOORS

Some parts of the ocean floor are more prone to volcanic activity than others. They are common along subduction zones, where ocean trenches are made (see pages 20–21). This can create a chain of volcanic islands, called an island arc. Other islands are created by small, very hot areas called hot spots, which can occur anywhere on tectonic plates if the crust is thin – such as the Hawaiian islands in the central Pacific.

DIVERSITY HOT SPOTS

Ocean islands can become important places for creating diversity among species. This diversity means that a variety of species end up playing different roles in their ecosystem. Remote islands, including Hawaii in the Pacific, may end up having many species that are found nowhere else in the world. This is why wildlife on oceanic islands tends to be more unique than that on continental islands closer to larger mainland.

The Galápagos red-lipped batfish is unique to the Galápagos Islands.

A unique species of butterflyfish, native to Easter Island.

GALÁPAGOS
ISLANDS
COLOMBIA
ECUADOR
PERU

GALÁPAGOS ISLANDS
EASTERN PACIFIC

The Galápagos Islands, off the coast of Ecuador, are around 2.5 million years old and were formed over a volcanic hot spot in the eastern Pacific. The first animals to colonize have evolved into unique species that only live here – such as Galápagos fur seals, flightless cormorants, and Galápagos blennies.

CORAL ATOLLS

Some of the most idyllic islands on Earth are bathed in tropical sunshine, surrounded by white beaches, and fringed by a clear blue lagoon and colorful coral reef. These coral atolls may, over time, be entirely built of layer upon layer of rocky coral. You can spot a coral atoll from its ring-shaped reef – the remnants of a long-extinct volcanic island.

TROPICAL CORALS

In tropical ocean waters, corals form some of the richest and most colorful ocean communities found anywhere on Earth. Around the rim of a volcanic island, where the light is bright and the waters are warm, conditions are perfect for corals to grow into big rocky reefs (see pages 96–97).

GROWING REEF

As the islands gradually sink (sometimes taking the coral with them), new coral will continue to grow. The coral colony will strive to stay near the sunlit surface, where the algae inside it can photosynthesize to help nourish the growing coral. For this to happen, the reef grows up toward the light, just like a plant.

Gorgonians are soft corals that grow in the shallow waters of Turneffe Atoll in the Caribbean Sea and feed on tiny plankton.

The reef grows thick around the edge, where waves bring plenty of nutrients.

THE VOLCANO EXTINGUISHES

If the volcanic activity that originally created an island stops, and no new rock erupts from its vent (this happens when the plate drifts away from the source of magma below it), weathering and erosion begin to wear the island away. Coral continues to thrive around the island's shores, often growing to form a fringing reef. A calm lagoon forms between the coral and the island in the middle.

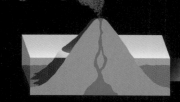

1. A volcanic island becomes extinct (stops erupting).

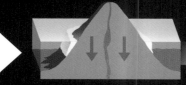

2. The island begins to wear away, but coral continues growing around the outer edge.

CONDITIONS ON AN ATOLL

Coral atolls take thousands or even millions of years to grow. As this happens, rich communities of life develop that are often unique to the habitat due to its isolated location. The calm of the inner atoll contrasts with the crashing ocean waves that strike the outer edge, providing a safe place for creatures to lay eggs and raise their young.

ORIGIN OF AN IDEA

The first person to devise a theory for how coral atolls form was the naturalist Charles Darwin, best known for his theory of evolution. In 1831, Darwin began a five-year-long voyage around the world, aboard the ship HMS *Beagle*. He witnessed many coral atolls firsthand and published his theory in 1842, making him well ahead of his time, as it wasn't proved correct until 1950 – over 100 years later!

Naturalist and geologist Charles Darwin (1809–1882)

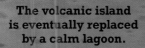

The inner edge of a coral atoll slopes down into a lagoon.

The volcanic island is eventually replaced by a calm lagoon.

LIFOU

AUSTRALIA

PACIFIC OCEAN

LIFOU
LOYALTY ISLANDS

Spanning an area of 442 sq. mi. (1,146 sq km), Lifou, in the Loyalty Islands of the southwest Pacific, is the largest coral atoll in the world. The natural geological movements of rock below the ocean bed have pushed the atoll upward, exposing high cliffs made from piles of long-dead coral rock.

FORMING AN ATOLL

The growing coral becomes a barrier reef, now separated from the shrinking island at its center by an increasingly wide lagoon. Eventually, the island erodes so much that it sinks below the surface of the ocean and only the ring of rocky coral remains: a coral atoll. Coral atolls, such as those in the Maldives, are among the smallest and lowest-lying of all of Earth's islands. Over time, sand and sediment settle on top of the rocky coral foundations.

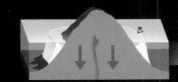

3. As the coral reef expands, a lagoon forms between the reef and the shrinking island.

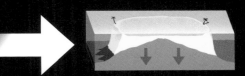

4. The island shrinks beneath the water, leaving the ring-shaped coral reef – an atoll.

POLAR SEAS

Earth's North and South Poles are harsh environments, where land and seas are permanently covered in ice and, at certain times of year, experience constant daylight or constant night. With freezing temperatures and seasonal extremes of light and dark, these regions provide some of the biggest challenges for life.

THE POLAR REGIONS

The polar regions are contained within the Arctic and Antarctic circles, and make up 16.5 percent of the planet's surface. These regions are defined as areas where, on at least one summer day, the Sun never sets and on at least one winter day, it never rises.

Low angle of incoming sunlight

Sunlight strikes most directly

SUN

Equator

Low angle of incoming sunlight

EARTH

THE ALBEDO EFFECT

When sunshine lands on the Earth, some of the Sun's rays are absorbed and warm the surface, while the rest are reflected and bounce off. Some surfaces reflect more sunlight than others – for example, light surfaces reflect more than dark surfaces – something called the albedo effect. This is why wearing white on a hot day keeps you cooler. Snow and ice reflect the most, which stops the snowy polar regions from warming up, so they stay cold.

The white coat of an Arctic fox blends into its frozen home.

WHY IS IT SO COLD?

At the equator, the Sun's rays strike the Earth head-on, concentrating their heat over a small area of land or sea, making it hotter. But in the polar regions, the rays strike the Earth at an angle, and this spreads the heat over a wider area, bringing less warmth. This makes water freeze and brings precipitation as snow.

NORTH POLE

POLAR ICE SHEETS

Earth's frozen poles are covered in huge expanses of very thick ice. At the North Pole, one enormous sheet covers Greenland, with an average thickness of 1.2 mi. (2 km). At the South Pole, two ice sheets cover Antarctica, separated by the Transantarctic Mountains. These sheets are up to 2.5 mi. (4 km) thick!

About **1.7%** of Earth's water is frozen into ice sheets at the poles.

SOUTH POLE

DAYLIGHT HOURS

At the equator, the length of the daytime is about the same as the length of the night – 12 hours of light are followed by 12 hours of dark. But as you get further away from the equator, the hours of daylight increase in the summer and decrease in the winter. These reach extremes at the poles, which experience nearly six months of constant summer sunshine and six months of winter darkness when the Sun never rises.

24-hour days in the Arctic

24-hour nights in the Arctic

SUMMER SOLSTICE (June 21)

WINTER SOLSTICE (Dec. 21)

LIVING AT THE POLES

All these factors come together to make challenging conditions for life in polar regions. Temperatures scarcely hover above freezing, even in summer. And for much of the year, the poles are in complete darkness, so photosynthesizing plants cannot grow year-round. The thick, floating ice also makes life more difficult for air-breathing animals that live mainly in the water.

Walruses have a thick layer of blubber to help them survive the cold.

GEOGRAPHIC NORTH POLE
ARCTIC OCEAN

The extreme polar conditions make life very difficult in polar regions. The exact location of the North Pole – the most northernmost point on Earth – is in the middle of the Arctic Ocean, where the water is over 13,000 ft. (4,000 m) deep. Camp Barneo is a Russian base built close to the North Pole. It has to be rebuilt every year as the ice is constantly drifting south, moving the base away from the North Pole.

RUSSIA

ARCTIC OCEAN

GEOGRAPHIC NORTH POLE

GREENLAND

CANADA

ARCTIC VERSUS ANTARCTIC

The Arctic and Antarctic regions are both places of cold seas, snow, and ice. But in many other ways, they are surprisingly different. The Arctic region in the north is centered around an ocean that is ice-covered for much of the year, whereas in the south, ocean life surrounds a continent: Antarctica.

In the Arctic, ice covers **2.7 MILLION MI²** **(7 MILLION KM²)** of ocean, growing to **5.8 MILLION MI²** **(15 MILLION KM²)** in winter.

Five major rivers flow from North America and Asia into the Arctic Ocean.

POLAR SEAS AND POLAR LAND

The Arctic Ocean is the smallest and shallowest ocean on Earth, but this doesn't make it any less dramatic. It is surrounded by the North American and Eurasian continents, where large rivers drain northward into the sea. At the South Pole, freshwater streams on Antarctica are largely melted snow and ice, called meltwater, that drain into the deeper Southern Ocean.

A WARMER ARCTIC

Temperatures in the Arctic do not dip as low as in the Antarctic. This is because water is continuously moving between the Arctic Ocean and North Atlantic Ocean, bringing warmer currents. Also, a layer of pack ice – compressed floating ice up to 40 ft. (12 m) thick – helps to trap heat in the Arctic Ocean underneath.

Ice reach in March

Ice reach in September

ARCTIC

Dense pack ice traps warmth in the ocean beneath.

COOLING THE DEEP

A global deep-water movement called the thermohaline circulation (see page 45) is responsible for carrying water between the equator and the poles. Warm water from the equator moves to the poles, where it cools, becomes denser and heavier, and plunges into the deep. This chilled water spreading out from Antarctica into the expanse of the Southern Ocean surrounding it is what keeps all the deep open oceans so cold.

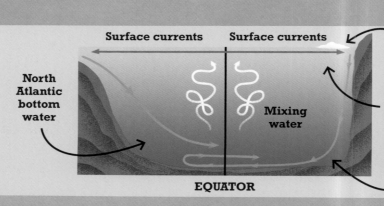

Surface currents

Surface currents

North Atlantic bottom water

Mixing water

Sea ice

Surface water cools and sinks.

Antarctic bottom water

EQUATOR

A COLDER ANTARCTIC

The foundation of Antarctica is a roughly circular continent, most of which is covered in snow. This reflects much of the Sun's radiation, giving it a higher albedo effect (see page 120). At the same time, the strong ocean current that flows around Antarctica, called the circumpolar current, makes it more difficult for warmer currents from the equator to reach its shores. Both factors cause temperatures to plunge to -129°F (-89.5°C) – the coldest recorded temperature on Earth.

Antarctic penguins huddle for warmth in bitter winds and snow.

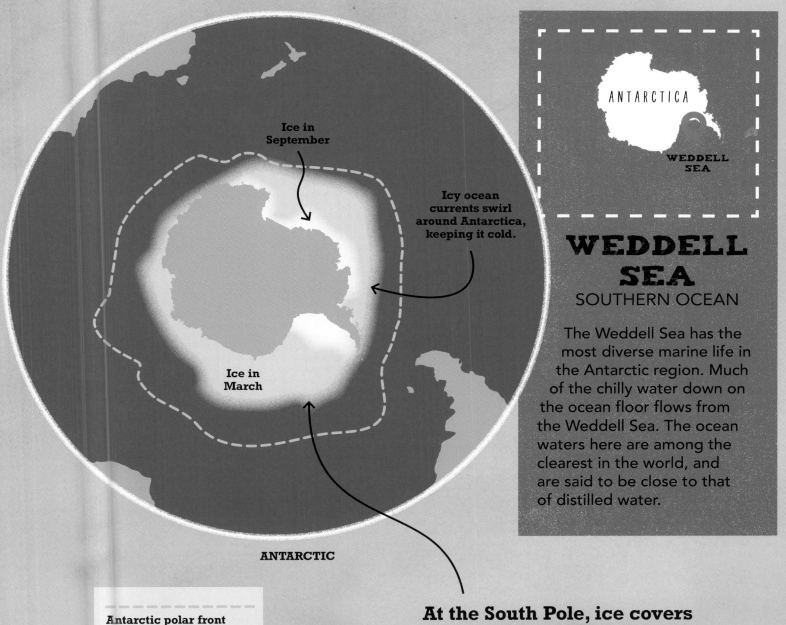

Ice in September

Icy ocean currents swirl around Antarctica, keeping it cold.

Ice in March

ANTARCTIC

- - - - - - -
Antarctic polar front

ANTARCTICA

WEDDELL SEA

WEDDELL SEA
SOUTHERN OCEAN

The Weddell Sea has the most diverse marine life in the Antarctic region. Much of the chilly water down on the ocean floor flows from the Weddell Sea. The ocean waters here are among the clearest in the world, and are said to be close to that of distilled water.

THE POLAR FRONT

Some of the chilled water coming from Antarctica returns northward on the surface of the Southern Ocean, then eventually sinks beneath the warmer (less dense) waters traveling from the equator. At this point, the climate becomes suddenly mild. This is called the polar front. Here, polar animals are replaced by temperate-zone animals, which are better suited to the milder climate.

At the South Pole, ice covers
**1 MILLION MI²
(3 MILLION KM²)** of the
Southern Ocean, growing to
**7 MILLION MI²
(18 MILLION KM²)** in winter.

SURVIVING POLAR SEAS

The organisms that live in the polar seas are very different from those found elsewhere in the oceans. Their adaptations have made them entirely dependent on the cold waters, meaning that many are able to live, grow, and breed in temperatures close to the freezing point. They now couldn't survive anywhere else!

LIFE IN THE SLOW LANE
Even before ice forms, lower temperatures can mean slower lives. All living things rely on chemical reactions in the body, called metabolism, to drive their vital functions – such as turning food into energy. These reactions slow down when it is colder because molecules have less energy and so move more slowly. As a result, for many animals, processes such as digestion and respiration are slower.

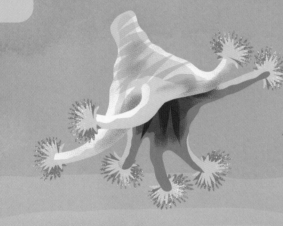

SOUTH
ATLANTIC
OCEAN

ZAVODOVSKI
ISLAND

Arctic stalked jellyfish live under the ice.

ZAVODOVSKI ISLAND
SOUTH ATLANTIC OCEAN

Animal life at the southern end of the world is largely concentrated on islands around Antarctica – away from the extremes of climate, but still bitterly cold. Zavodovski Island, northeast of the Antarctic peninsula, is home to nearly 2 million chinstrap penguins – the largest colony of penguins outside the Antarctic continent.

Elephant seals have thick, protective blubber for warmth.

TRAPPING BODY HEAT
Warm-blooded animals of polar seas – including orcas, whales, seals, and penguins – are able to stay active even though they live in very cold habitats because they generate their own heat (see opposite). But such a big temperature difference between inside and outside their body also needs good insulation – a method to stop too much heat from escaping. Many animals have thick fatty layers, called blubber, beneath their skin.

WORK SLOW, LIVE LONG

A sluggish metabolism can mean that growth and reproduction are slow, too. Slow bodies need less fuel, so predators in the polar oceans may only need to catch one decent meal every few weeks to survive. Slow-growing bodies also wear out less quickly, so they live longer. The Greenland shark of Arctic waters can live for literally hundreds of years!

Scientists discovered a Greenland shark that might have been over 500 years old!

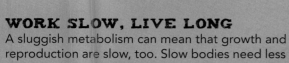

Whooper swans migrate to and from Arctic breeding grounds.

AVOIDING THE COLD

One way of coping with the most extreme polar cold is to avoid it altogether! Shorebirds that breed on Arctic coastlines in summer fly south to milder climates before the harsh winter sets in. And some whales that come to the Arctic to feed soon start their journey south, where they breed in warmer waters near the equator.

Starfish live under the ice.

ANTIFREEZING BODIES

The bodies of all living things contain water, which means if they get too cold, their tissues can freeze solid. Very few kinds of polar animals can tolerate even partial freezing – for most, the ice crystals would damage their cells and could kill them. But many polar organisms, including some fish and plants on land, contain antifreeze chemicals in their blood that stop these ice crystals from forming.

Notothenioid fish contain antifreeze in their blood to stop them freezing.

COUNTERCURRENT EXCHANGERS

Extremities, like the legs and feet of a penguin, are especially vulnerable to losing heat. To help reduce this, they often have a special arrangement of blood vessels. Blood flowing away from the body's core – its hottest part – transfers heat to closely aligned vessels, carrying cooler blood back, away from extremities. In this way, less heat is lost to the icy ground, or to water during a dive.

Leopard seals generate their own heat, helping them hunt in polar seas.

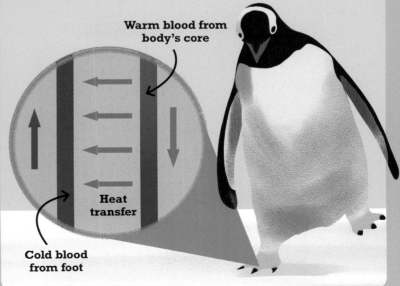

Warm blood from body's core

Heat transfer

Cold blood from foot

GENERATING BODY HEAT

Most kinds of organisms, including plants, invertebrates, and fish, are ectotherms. This means that they rely on their surroundings to absorb heat. Their bodies generate so little heat themselves that they usually match the temperature of their surroundings. But birds and mammals are endotherms: they can generate their own heat so they can maintain a body temperature that is higher than the environment around them.

FROZEN SEAS

Unsurprisingly, there is a lot of ice in the polar regions. Ice sheets hold 90 percent of Earth's freshwater (water that isn't salty) and expand far out over the oceans in winter. But climate change is threatening Earth's frozen seas, which are warming faster than anywhere else.

FREEZING SEAWATER

Salt drops the freezing point of water to below 32°F (0°C), so most seawater freezes at just above 28°F (-2°C). In the Arctic, where waters are slightly less salty, the freezing point is just a little bit higher. Ice forms from tiny crystals of solidified (frozen) water. Salt doesn't freeze, so as the ice crystals bond together, the salt is left behind, and pockets of concentrated salt form within the ice.

Tiny ice crystals make intricate patterns as they bond.

Icebergs are huge chunks of ice that have broken off a glacier or ice shelf.

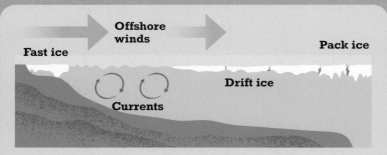

Offshore winds

Fast ice

Pack ice

Drift ice

Currents

SEA ICE

When ice forms in polar seas, it floats, because ice is less dense than water. Much of this is called fast ice, meaning it is connected (or fastened) to the land and does not move. Other ice is made at sea, and because it moves with winds and currents, it is called drift ice. Floating chunks of drift ice can collect together in large masses – called pack ice.

Thin Arctic sea ice over a calm ocean. Climate change is melting Arctic sea ice at a rapid rate.

ARCTIC VS. ANTARCTIC PACK ICE

Sea ice gets broken up by the buffeting action of ocean currents, but in the enclosed Arctic Ocean, conditions are calm enough for pack ice to grow much thicker. The choppier waters of the Southern Ocean stop most of the sea ice from developing, so it is thinner.

Dazzling "blue icebergs" are made of compressed glacial ice that looks blue as the light bounces off it.

WHEN ICE DRIFTS LONG DISTANCES

Floating drift ice can be carried over long distances by ocean currents, sometimes traveling several miles a day. Huge icy chunks that break away from polar ice sheets are called icebergs. They tower over 16 ft. (5 m) above sea level – but icebergs reach much deeper below the surface. Nearly 90 percent of their total size is hidden underwater!

SHRINKING GIANTS

As drifting ice approaches warmer water, it melts, but some chunks are so big that they last a long time. Iceberg B-15 is the largest recorded to date: it was the size of Jamaica when it broke away from the Antarctic ice shelf in the year 2000! In 2018, a fragment of it was still floating in the South Atlantic.

DANGERS OF FLOATING ICE

For many air-breathing animals, swimming beneath the ice can be a potential danger as they could get trapped! Weddell seals grind their teeth against the ice to keep air holes open. Whales use brute force, bashing the ice until it breaks so they can reach the air above. Narwhals rely on natural gaps in the ice, called leads, where they surface and breathe. These methods don't always work though, and many animals drown if pack ice freezes over too quickly.

BENEFITS OF FLOATING ICE

Many Arctic seals, such as harp seals and ringed seals, rely on floating ice as safe places to give birth or rest away from predators. Similarly, floating ice can provide shelter for smaller animals that hide below the ocean surface. In Antarctica, krill – the most abundant kind of zooplankton – gather in huge numbers beneath the ice, where they graze on algae that grow between the water crystals.

Krill are only 2.5 in. (6 cm) long but are a main food source for whales and penguins.

NORTH WATER POLYNYA
ARCTIC OCEAN

A polynya is a stretch of open polar ocean, surrounded by sea ice, that provides an important refuge for many animals. The largest Arctic polynya is in northern Baffin Bay, dubbed the "North Water" by whalers of the 1800s. It is a place where many mammals, including narwhals, walruses, and bowhead whales, can rest and feed throughout the year.

GREENLAND

NORTH WATER POLYNYA

BAFFIN BAY

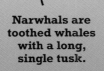

Narwhals are toothed whales with a long, single tusk.

Narwhals are also known as "the unicorns of the sea."

NAVIGATION

Humans have been swimming and sailing in the oceans since prehistoric times – and some even embarked on overseas journeys that covered thousands of miles. But it took breakthroughs in technology and science to help make navigation as reliable as it is today.

SETTING OUT TO SEA

As Stone Age people living along the coasts explored their surroundings, they may have built the first boats from hollowed tree trunks – called dugouts. As long ago as 50,000 BCE, people from Southeast Asia crossed deep ocean water in simple boats to arrive in New Guinea and Australia, making them among the first long-distance sailors. By 2300 BCE, their descendants had colonized islands of the Pacific. These early navigators used their knowledge of currents and the position of the Sun and stars to help them find their way.

An ancient compass found in a Chinese shipwreck. When the bowl is full of water, it floats, and the needle points south.

THE MAGNETIC COMPASS

Figuring out the relative position or direction of a boat using the Sun and stars works well in clear weather, but not when it gets cloudy! The first compasses, invented in China over 2,000 years ago, solved this problem. They were made from thin pieces of lodestone – a magnetic mineral that aligns itself with the Earth's magnetic field to point north and south.

FIRST NAVIGATION

A compass shows direction, but cannot pinpoint position. For this, people needed to develop a system of global coordinates, and the ancient Greeks were the first to figure this out. Their system involved dividing the Earth up into lines of latitude and longitude, and position was described by where these lines crossed on a map – like an invisible grid.

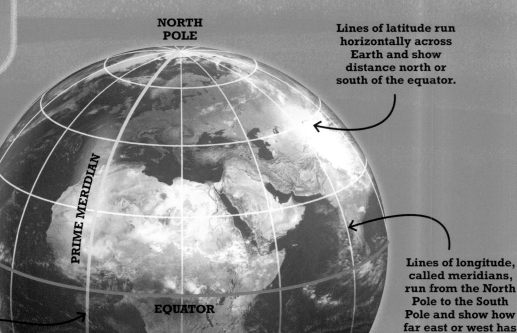

NORTH POLE

PRIME MERIDIAN

EQUATOR

Lines of latitude run horizontally across Earth and show distance north or south of the equator.

Lines of longitude, called meridians, run from the North Pole to the South Pole and show how far east or west has been traveled.

The prime meridian runs from the North Pole to the South Pole and marks 0° longitude (see opposite).

Ancient Polynesian sailors memorized the positions of the Sun, stars, and land to find their way, perhaps as early as 1200 BCE.

USING SIGNALS

As technology advanced, navigation at sea improved. In the 1900s, devices were invented for detecting radio waves from distant transmitters. By knowing the location of two transmitters, the position of a ship could be calculated. Later, radar helped boats detect the position of other boats and land nearby – radar devices transmit radio waves that bounce off objects, revealing their positions. Since the 1980s, when satellites were launched into space, navigation has improved greatly. These satellites continuously transmit radio signals and are used to figure out the position of anything on Earth with a receiver – including ships at sea. It was named the "Global Positioning System" (GPS) and is still used by vessels today.

MEASURING LATITUDE AND LONGITUDE

Latitude came from measuring the angle between the Sun or stars and the horizon, using a sextant. Longitude could only be found by comparing time differences in positions around the world. Keeping time at sea was difficult because old-fashioned clocks had swinging pendulums, and the pendulum would often be knocked out of sync by the motion of the waves. In 1759, clockmaker John Harrison invented a clock that was so accurate, it could calculate how much time was lost or gained by going east or west. This helped figure out longitude.

Sextant

Captain James Cook used one of Harrison's clocks on his first voyage around the world.

There are at least eight GPS satellites in the sky above you at any one time.

GREENWICH
LONDON, UNITED KINGDOM

Following the invention of seaworthy clocks, British ships always kept one clock fixed at the time in Greenwich, London, as a reference to help follow time differences as ships moved further west or east. In 1884, the Greenwich prime meridian – a line drawn from the North Pole to the South Pole through Greenwich – was officially accepted as zero degrees longitude.

ATLANTIC OCEAN

GREENWICH

U K

EUROPE

OCEAN SCIENCE

Oceanography is a branch of science that uses different techniques to study everything about the oceans – from the depths of its floors and the movement of its crust to the flow of its currents and the rich and diverse habitat it provides for living things.

THE BIRTH OF OCEAN SCIENCE

In 1855, an American scientist called Matthew Maury published a textbook entitled *The Physical Geography of the Sea*, in which he described the geography of the oceans and the effects of their currents. It was the most thorough study of the oceans ever published and is why Maury is known as the "father of oceanography."

Matthew Maury was an astronomer and oceanographer (1806–1873).

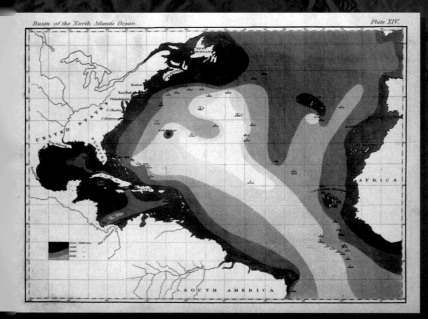

The earliest bathymetric map of an ocean basin, which shows distance to the ocean floor (depth), was published in 1853.

MAPPING THE SEABED

Maury lacked the technology needed to study the seabed directly, so instead he studied the information recorded by ships' logs. These logs were made during voyages in different parts of the world. Information about depths, winds, and currents was recorded using a range of simple instruments; for example, a line of material with a weight at the end was used to measure depth. By putting all of the information together for the first time, he discovered that a mid-ocean ridge ran down through the Atlantic Ocean.

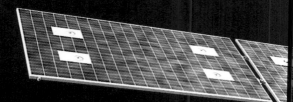

Maury released wind and current charts for the Atlantic and Indian Oceans in 1860.

TIDES, WINDS, AND CURRENTS

The link between tides and the positions of the Moon and Sun had first been made by ancient philosophers in Greece and Babylonia. As people began exploring the world by ship from the 1500s onward, navigators recorded how winds pushed water along particular routes. Their observations helped Maury and other oceanographers map the currents of the world's oceans (see pages 44–45). These routes were relied on in trading and war.

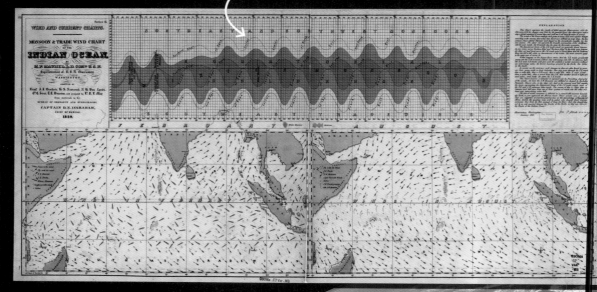

MOVING FLOORS

As science progressed, people went on to discover how oceans changed over time. In the 1960s, an American geologist called Harry Hess suggested that the Mid-Atlantic Ridge, first detected by Maury, was a place where the seafloor was spreading. Hess's theory supported the idea that the continents had drifted slowly over millions of years, but this was mostly ridiculed at the time.

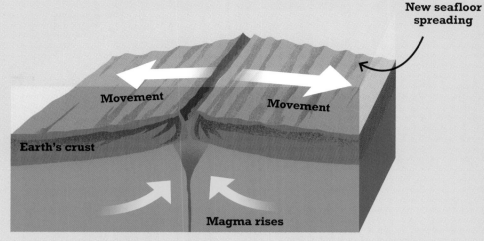

New seafloor spreading

Movement

Movement

Earth's crust

Magma rises

At either side of an oceanic ridge, the patterns of rock are symmetrical, showing that new seafloor spreads away from the ridge on both sides.

Geologist Harry Hess (1906–1969)

EXCAVATING THE DEEP SEA

In the 1970s, research ships got even closer to the mysterious ocean floor – by drilling down and taking samples of its rocks. Deep-sea drilling was difficult, but the samples collected revealed some extraordinary things. They showed, for instance, that nowhere on Earth was the ocean floor older than 180 million years, and that new bed was continually being made – just as Harry Hess had suggested was happening around the Mid-Atlantic Ridge.

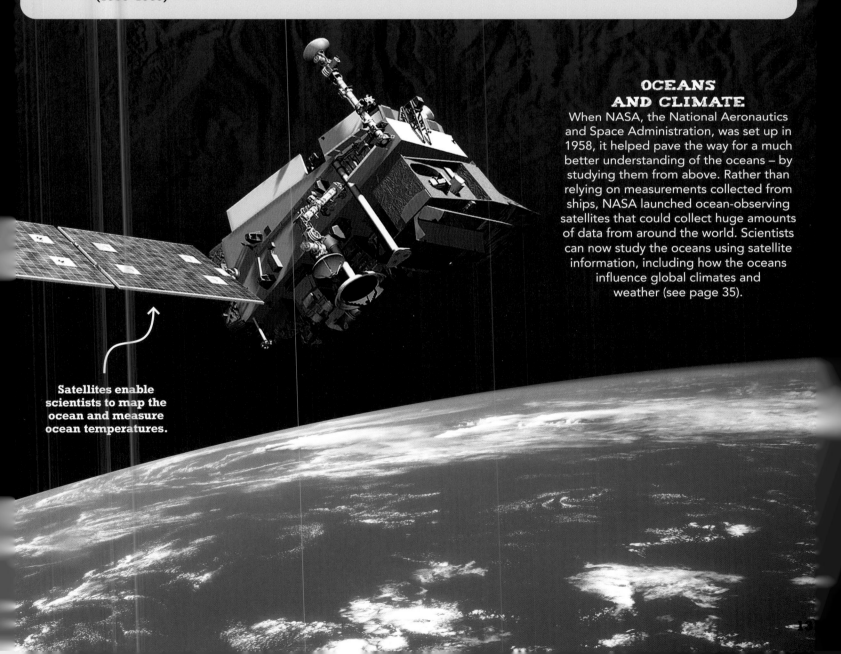

OCEANS AND CLIMATE

When NASA, the National Aeronautics and Space Administration, was set up in 1958, it helped pave the way for a much better understanding of the oceans – by studying them from above. Rather than relying on measurements collected from ships, NASA launched ocean-observing satellites that could collect huge amounts of data from around the world. Scientists can now study the oceans using satellite information, including how the oceans influence global climates and weather (see page 35).

Satellites enable scientists to map the ocean and measure ocean temperatures.

DISCOVERING NEW LIFE

Every year, scientists discover new kinds of plants and creatures, and many of these discoveries are made in the world's seas. As scientists are able to reach further into the deepest, least explored parts of the ocean, they are finding many remarkable living things that are unlike anything seen ever before.

HOW MANY SPECIES?

There are around 1.5 million known species alive today. Most of these are animals and the rest include microbes, algae, fungi, and plants. About a third of these organisms live in the oceans. But scientists believe that this is just a fraction of the total number on Earth. It is thought that more than 80 percent are yet to be discovered – largely because there are just so many to study!

WHERE ARE THEY HIDING?

Many new species are found in the least explored parts of the ocean, especially the deep sea, which is difficult to travel to even today. But new species are also being discovered in easily reachable places: along coastlines, in coral reefs, and in shallow seas. There is so much diversity in living things that new species can even be found in a cupful of plankton scooped up from the ocean surface.

A marine biologist takes a sample of ocean water.

Megamouth sharks are rarely sighted by humans.

At 16.5 ft. (5 m) long, and with a gaping mouth, these sharks are pretty mega!

SPECTACULAR DISCOVERIES

The oceans are so massive that they provide new species with plenty of space to hide, and not just small creatures. The huge, filter-feeding megamouth shark was not discovered until 1976, and in 1997, zoologists identified an Indonesian coelacanth. This relative of the first vertebrates to crawl on land was thought to be extinct, but was found among the catch at a fish market (see page 70).

CURAÇAO
THE CARIBBEAN

In 2018, scientists exploring reefs around the Caribbean island of Curaçao discovered a new kind of habitat, where one in five species of fish is new. This deep-water reef system, which they called the rariphotic (meaning "scarce light") zone, occurs 425–985 ft. (130–300 m) below the surface – deeper than any other known reef habitat.

CARIBBEAN SEA

CURAÇAO

SOUTH AMERICA

BIOLOGICAL EXPLORATION

Many species are discovered on expeditions to places where diversity is known to be especially rich, and hundreds of new species of crustaceans, snails, and fish can be found. Altogether, a vast total of 416 new species of fish were recorded in 2018 alone – so there's always more to discover!

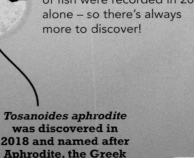

Tosanoides aphrodite was discovered in 2018 and named after Aphrodite, the Greek goddess of love.

DESCRIBING NEW SPECIES

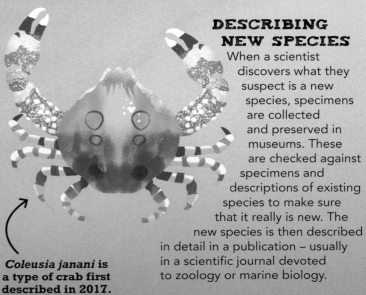

When a scientist discovers what they suspect is a new species, specimens are collected and preserved in museums. These are checked against specimens and descriptions of existing species to make sure that it really is new. The new species is then described in detail in a publication – usually in a scientific journal devoted to zoology or marine biology.

Coleusia janani is a type of crab first described in 2017.

Cirrhilabrus wakanda was discovered hiding over 200 ft. (60 m) deep.

SOURCES OF NAMES

Scientists often name new species after places, people, and other sources of inspiration. In 2019, a colorful fairy wrasse caught off Africa was named *Cirrhilabrus wakanda*. *Cirrhilabrus* is the genus name for fairy wrasses, and *wakanda*, the species name, was inspired by the fictional African kingdom of Wakanda from Marvel Comics' superhero stories, *Black Panther*. In the stories, Wakanda is named after a rare purple metal, which is similar in color to this little purple fish.

NAMING SPECIES

The new species is given a two-part scientific name in Latin. The first part, called the genus name (like a surname that links a family), refers to a group of closely related species. The second part is unique to one specific species. For instance, the genus name *Carcharhinus* is used for more than 30 species of related reef sharks. Within this group, *Carcharhinus galapagensis* is the Galápagos reef shark and *Carcharhinus melanopterus* is the blacktip reef shark.

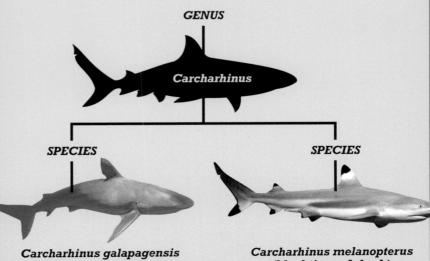

GENUS

Carcharhinus

SPECIES

SPECIES

Carcharhinus galapagensis (Galápagos reef shark)

Carcharhinus melanopterus (blacktip reef shark)

DIVING

With practice, humans can become expert swimmers and divers, although plunging into the ocean depths brings extreme challenges that go beyond just holding your breath. Developments in science and technology have helped divers go deeper, stay submerged for longer, and explore further than ever before.

FREE DIVING

Diving underwater without the use of any breathing equipment is called free diving. The diver must hold their breath, during which time the body uses up oxygen and accumulates carbon dioxide, both of which eventually force the diver to surface for air. Russian diver Alexey Molchanov holds the world record for deepest self-propelled dive – diving to a depth of 423 ft. (129 m) for 3 minutes 50 seconds.

IMPROVING PERFORMANCE

Human feet aren't particularly well designed for swimming underwater. To help divers swim faster, they wear fins called flippers on their feet, which push against the water, propelling them forward. A diving mask – either full face mask or a half-mask that only covers the eyes – helps divers to focus normally by looking through a pocket of air without water getting into their eyes.

Diving masks allow divers to see normally.

Snorkeling is a fun and easy way to explore underwater habitats close to the shore.

SNORKELING

Some face masks are fitted with a breathing tube called a snorkel. These help swimmers near the surface to breathe while their faces are underwater. Snorkeling is a great way to explore areas where the water is clear, such as coral reefs. In shallow underwater habitats, snorkelers can swim among colorful coral and darting fish, while still breathing – so they can stay underwater for longer.

Flippers allow divers to swim faster using less energy.

The breathing tube connects to an air compressor at the surface.

SURFACE-SUPPLIED DIVING

The simplest equipment that helps divers to breathe down to about 23 ft. (7 m) deep is a long hose-like breathing tube that connects to an air supply at the surface, either from the shore or from a boat. The tube fits to a full face mask or to a valve held in the mouth. This kind of surface-supplied diving is useful for underwater activities that do not have to stray far from the source of the air supply, such as archaeological or scientific research.

SCUBA

Scuba diving allows divers to swim underwater without being tethered to land. Instead, they carry with them a supply of air to breathe, usually as compressed air contained in cylinders. This technology is called a self-contained underwater breathing apparatus (SCUBA), and is usually strapped to the diver's back. Scuba divers receive special training before they are allowed to use the equipment, which can take them to 131–197 ft. (40–60 m) deep.

Scuba divers wear a cylinder of compressed air connected to a valve held in the mouth.

ATMOSPHERIC PRESSURE DIVING

The furthest that a person can dive outside a diving vehicle is 2,000 ft. (610 m). To reach such depths, a diver needs an atmospheric pressure diving suit (a bit like a suit of armor!), along with a source of breathable air that can last four hours. The suit keeps the diver dry and at the same pressure as at the surface, so that they are not crushed by the higher pressure deep underwater.

Atmospheric pressure divers look more like astronauts wearing space suits!

UNDERWATER VEHICLES

Although technology allows people to develop the safest possible ways to dive, there are always risks involved when venturing into places that humans aren't designed for! The main difficulties to overcome are the lack of air (risk of drowning) and the pressure change as you travel deeper. Some places are just too deep or difficult to get to, so to explore depths that go beyond the limits of diving suits, divers rely on specially designed underwater vehicles (see page 136).

SUBMERSIBLES

Underwater craft can travel further and deeper than human divers, even when humans are supported by specialized suits. Some of these are unmanned (no one is inside) and are operated by a remote-control robot. Others, called submersibles, usually carry one or two human passengers, enabling scientists to reach the very deepest parts of the ocean (see pages 106–113).

WHAT IS A SUBMERSIBLE?

Some underwater vessels, such as submarines, can recharge batteries and renew air supplies onboard, so they can stay underwater for long periods of time. Unlike a submarine, a submersible is launched from a boat and relies on it for support – such as an air supply delivered through a tube. Some of these submersibles are so strong that they can withstand the pressures involved in diving to the very deepest parts of the ocean.

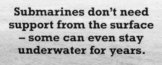

Submarines don't need support from the surface – some can even stay underwater for years.

Submersibles are usually built for one or two passengers, but submarines can hold many more.

SUPPORTING PASSENGERS

If a submersible is to carry human passengers (and allow them to breathe and talk without special equipment), it must enclose them in a capsule of air that is kept at the same pressure as air at the surface. Sometimes, the submersible is connected to a surface support vessel through a breathing tube, which is given the name "umbilicus" (after the life-giving cord that connects a baby to its mother in the womb). The occupants can steer their craft by controlling propellers or water jets that shoot out behind it.

RESISTING THE PRESSURE

Manned submersibles have descended to the very deepest parts of the ocean – around 6.2 mi. (10 km) deep! To do so, they must withstand the huge pressure difference between the outside and inside of the vessel, where atmospheric pressure is maintained for those inside. Without these precautions, the submersible would be crushed by the extreme pressures. A submersible is typically made from titanium, a very strong metal that is not corroded by seawater.

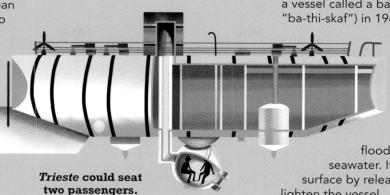

The bathyscaphe, *Trieste.*

Trieste could seat two passengers.

CONTROLLING DEPTH

The first submersible to reach the deepest part of the ocean, the Mariana Trench, was a vessel called a bathyscaphe (pronounced "ba-thi-skaf") in 1960. Piloted by Dan Walsh and Jacques Piccard, son of the vessel's inventor, the bathyscaphe, named *Trieste*, descended to a depth of more than 35,813 ft. (10,916 m) by gradually flooding its air tanks with seawater. It later rose back to the surface by releasing iron weights to lighten the vessel.

BREAKING THE RECORD

In May 2019, the American underwater explorer Victor Vescovo – piloting a new submersible called the DSV *Limiting Factor* – went even deeper than Walsh and Piccard, the previous record-holders. It reached 35,853 ft. (10,928 m) down into the Mariana Trench and has also explored trenches in other parts of the world – including in the Atlantic, Southern, and Indian Oceans.

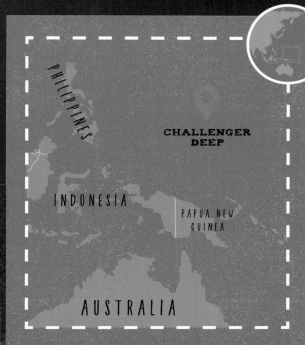

CHALLENGER DEEP

PHILIPPINES

INDONESIA

PAPUA NEW GUINEA

AUSTRALIA

CHALLENGER DEEP
MARIANA TRENCH

At around 36,000 ft. (10,990 m), Challenger Deep in the western Pacific Ocean is the deepest place anywhere in the ocean. Life here has adapted to survive pressures that are 100 times greater than at sea level. Despite being so difficult to reach, man-made waste is found even here, showing the scale of damage that humans are inflicting on the oceans.

EXPLORING THE DEEP

Modern submersibles are equipped with lots of technology to help those onboard explore the deep. Lighting helps to illuminate the dark depths of the ocean, while additional onboard equipment, like photo and video cameras, helps scientists to record their findings. Some submersibles even have mechanical arms to help collect samples of organisms to study later at the surface.

SHIPWRECKS

It is little wonder that shipwrecks attract a lot of attention from divers. They offer fascinating snapshots of the past for people interested in history, and sometimes even the promise of sunken treasure! Shipwrecks can be filled with things from a bygone age that can be recovered and carefully preserved in museums.

WHAT IS A SHIPWRECK?

Any ship that has sunk beneath the waves, or beached – when a boat gets stuck in shallow water closer to shore – becomes a shipwreck. This can happen by accident, such as when ships collide with rocks or icebergs, or by deliberate action, such as during wartime battles. It is thought that around the world there are about 3 million shipwrecks, and most are hidden far below the ocean surface.

Shipwrecks offer nooks and crannies for divers to explore!

A huge team of scientists, archaeologists, and divers worked to salvage the *Mary Rose* over many years.

HISTORICAL SHIPWRECKS

Ancient shipwrecks can tell historians a lot about the past. Everything left on board gives information about the way the people of the time lived their lives, as well as specific events – such as sea battles. Great efforts are made to preserve ancient shipwrecks, such as the *Mary Rose* – an English warship belonging to King Henry VIII. The *Mary Rose* sank in the 1500s off the south coast of England but was discovered in 1971 and is now on display in Portsmouth, UK.

STATE OF PRESERVATION

Lots of factors determine how well a shipwreck is preserved over time. Organic materials, like wood, rot away because decomposers such as bacteria and ocean worms feed on them, while metal corrodes and rusts as it reacts with seawater. Wrecks stay preserved for longer in colder waters, where they decompose slower, and in calmer places, where they are less buffeted by currents and waves.

Pewter plates were among the artifacts discovered in the *Mary Rose* shipwreck.

SHIPWRECKS AND POLLUTION

Shipwrecks eventually break down as their parts rot underwater, but this can pose a danger to the ocean environment. Vessels might carry materials that will pollute the waters, such as oil or plastic. Modern ships that sink are of special concern because they are more likely to carry harmful polluting substances that will have immediate effects on the surrounding seas.

Today, emergency teams respond quickly to lessen the environmental damage.

Shipwrecks are lifted to the surface, if possible. If not, hazardous materials are removed.

SALVAGE AND OWNERSHIP

When a shipwreck (or its parts) is rescued from the sea, it is called a salvage operation and involves specialized teams and equipment. The question of who owns a wreck can be difficult to answer, because the original owners of old vessels may no longer exist! Governments, archaeologists, and museums work together to decide whether to carefully raise the shipwreck to the surface or make it safer by removing harmful materials.

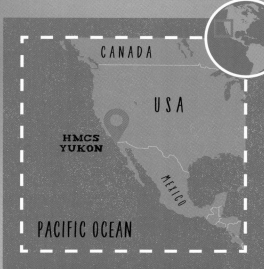

CANADA

USA

HMCS YUKON

MEXICO

PACIFIC OCEAN

DELIBERATE WRECKS

Sometimes, shipwrecks can actually be good news for marine life. In recent years, scientists have recognized that wrecks can provide important habitats for living things in the ocean. Today, some old vessels that are otherwise only useful for scrap have been stripped of their polluting parts and deliberately sunk to encourage coral reefs to grow.

Shipwrecks provide habitats for corals and other creatures.

MISSION BAY
CALIFORNIA, USA

After it was decommissioned from service in 2000, the Canadian Navy training ship HMCS *Yukon* was cleaned and deliberately sunk in Mission Bay off the coast of San Diego, California. Here, it provided the framework for the growth of a new coral reef and remains an important habitat for ocean wildlife.

SUCCESSION ON A SHIPWRECK

The framework of a shipwreck is like an artificial system of caves, providing a sheltered habitat where communities of species build up over time. First, animals as diverse as sharks, octopuses, and moray eels move in. Gradually, larvae of corals and barnacles settle on the surfaces of the shipwreck. These grow into colonies and eventually become a colorful reef that supports other types of life. This is an example of underwater succession in action (see page 116).

UNDERWATER CITIES

Deep underwater, hidden from view, lie lost cities full of ancient artifacts and treasures waiting to be found. Lost cities are places of great archaeological interest and are scattered all around the world. In times gone by – when these cities stood above the water – they were bustling with people. Now, hidden beneath the waves, their buildings make homes for ocean animals instead.

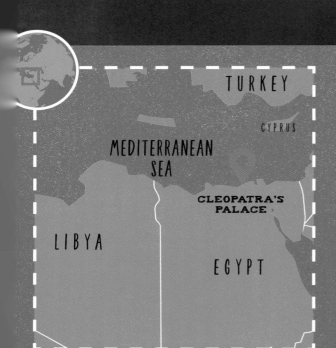

TURKEY

CYPRUS

MEDITERRANEAN
SEA

CLEOPATRA'S
PALACE

LIBYA

EGYPT

CLEOPATRA'S UNDERWATER PALACE
EGYPT

The palace of Cleopatra, the ancient Egyptian queen, was on a royal island off the coast of Alexandria in Egypt – until it was hit by an earthquake more than 1,500 years ago. The palace was huge and lavish, complete with sphinxes and a temple to the goddess Isis, before it sank 16 ft. (5 m) below the waters of the eastern Mediterranean. Today, divers can explore the remains of the lost city, seeing stone sphinxes, statues of goddesses, and the red granite columns that had welcomed visitors to the city. Above water, a museum of the site is also planned.

WHY CITIES SINK

Historical cities and towns on the coast may have sunk below the waves for various reasons. Often, they disappear underwater because of some sort of natural event, such as an earthquake, a tsunami, or coastal erosion that causes land to crumble into the sea. The ancient trading city of Simena, off the coast of modern-day Turkey, sank in the second century because of devastating earthquakes.

The ancient houses and harbor of Simena still exist today!

A map of Port Royal before the earthquake in 1692.

PORT ROYAL

Port Royal, Jamaica, was once the largest city in the Caribbean. From the 1500s, it was a bustling port for trade and shipping, and notorious for pirate activity. But in 1692, a great earthquake struck the region, which resulted in two-thirds of the city sinking into the sea. Today, it is a popular site for divers, eager to explore its secrets. In 1959, underwater archaeologist Edwin Link found a pocket watch with the time stopped at 11:43. It is thought that this was the time of the disaster.

The rock formations are a popular place to spot hammerhead sharks.

YONAGUNI MONUMENT

Sometimes, underwater sites might not be all they seem. Another popular diving spot is a rock formation called the Yonaguni Monument off the coast of Japan's Ryukyu Islands. Some people believe that the terraced blocks of stone look too regular to be rock that has formed naturally and that they are instead part of a man-made pyramid built at the time of the last ice age! But there is currently no agreement on what this formation really is.

ATLANTIS

The lost city of Atlantis was first mentioned in the writings of the ancient Greek philosopher Plato. It was said to have been situated on an island in the Atlantic or Mediterranean and has been a popular topic in stories ever since. But the legend of Atlantis is most likely just that: a story. It has never been found and there is no firm evidence that a city like this ever did exist.

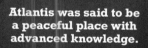

Atlantis was said to be a peaceful place with advanced knowledge.

UNDERWATER CITIES OF THE FUTURE

Cities submerged by water would seem to be doomed as places for humans to live, but modern technology is bringing the prospect of underwater buildings closer to reality. Already, it is possible to stay in hotels or dine in restaurants that are built partially under the sea. A Japanese company is planning to go a step further by building a modern-day Atlantis called Ocean Spiral. This underwater city could be home to 5,000 people and powered by energy extracted from the deep-sea floor, around 2.5 mi. (4 km) below. It is thought that the technology needed might be ready in around 15 years' time!

FISHING AND WHALING

Ever since prehistoric humans discovered that creatures in the oceans and along the shoreline could be used as food, they have fished the waters. Today, we use technology to maximize how much fish and seafood we can catch and are fishing on a bigger scale than ever before. But many of these methods are putting wild populations of ocean animals at risk, and even driving some to extinction.

WHAT IS FISHING?

The term "fishing" means hunting and catching fish, either for fun or for food. But fish aren't the only animals that are "fished" – snails, crabs, and shrimps all form part of a fisherman's catch. There are many different ways to fish, too – most of which are very far removed from traditional methods, such as using a rod and fishing line.

Spearfishing involves using sharpened sticks to hunt fish.

TRADITIONAL FISHING METHODS

People in ancient times developed many techniques for catching marine animals, some of which are still used locally around the world. There are four traditional methods that have stood the test of time: fish are hunted in shallow waters with spears, called spearfishing, or traps might be set to catch animals such as lobsters – called trapping. Angling involves catching fish on hooks on the end of fishing lines. And bigger catches are possible by sweeping the water with nets – called netting.

GREENLAND

CANADA

USA

GRAND BANKS

NORTH ATLANTIC

GRAND BANKS
NEWFOUNDLAND, CANADA

The Grand Banks are underwater plateaus off the east Canadian coast. With nutrient-rich waters, the area once provided some of the richest fishing grounds anywhere in the world. But overfishing caused populations of Atlantic cod to drop to just 1 percent of what it had been historically, forcing Grand Banks to close in 1992. Atlantic cod became listed as vulnerable to extinction as there were almost no adult fish left.

Stilt-fishing is a method of fishing that is unique to Sri Lanka.

NET FISHING

Nets in the water are used to catch lots of fish or other marine animals at once. Seine nets, which are weighed down with heavy materials such as stones, hang vertically in the water from boats or across a stretch of seashore to trap anything that swims into them. The size of the net's mesh depends on the prey that is being targeted – the smaller the prey, the smaller the gaps need to be to catch them.

Seine nets float and can be closed at the bottom, trapping fish.

SUSTAINABLE CATCHES

Modern fishing and hunting methods are so effective and catch so many creatures at a time that they are driving many ocean species close to extinction. Extinction happens when animals are killed faster than they are able to reproduce to replace the animals lost. Sustainable fishing is a way of trying to ensure that this does not happen – by fixing limits called quotas on the amount of fishing that can take place.

WHALING

Whales have been hunted with a type of long spear called a harpoon since prehistoric times, usually for their meat or oil, which was valued as a source of fuel. Hunting has seen populations of slow-breeding whales rapidly decline, and in the twentieth century, many species were driven close to extinction. This led the International Whaling Commission (IWC) to ban commercial whaling in 1986, which stops people hunting whales and selling whale products. In some places, such as Greenland, the hunting of whales by indigenous people is still allowed but is carefully managed.

People have been hunting whales for thousands of years.

Trawler nets collect huge quantities of fish at once.

TRAWLING

Trawlers are boats that pull a net behind them through the water. The net, called a trawl, is shaped like a giant basket, and traps fish and other sea creatures as it is dragged along. Trawls can catch huge amounts of fish at once, so are efficient, but can also be very damaging to the environment. Dragging a trawl net along the sea bottom destroys habitats, such as reefs, as the net drags up anything in its path – including creatures that are not the intended targets, such as anemones, starfish, and juvenile fish that are too small to be sold as food.

ENERGY AND MINERAL RESOURCES

The oceans provide us with more than just seafood, they are also a source of many precious natural resources. These resources are produced by the environment and provide us with energy to fuel our homes and transportation systems, and manufacture products. Oil and gas reservoirs (where natural resources collect) are often found deep beneath the ocean, stored in rocks in the seabed.

FUEL FROM THE DEEP

Most of the world's naturally occurring oil and gas is trapped in rocks under the ocean. Both oil and gas were formed hundreds of millions of years ago from the remains of dead plankton, which had sunk to the ocean bottom. Over millions of years, their remains were buried under layers of sediment, heated by warmth from Earth's mantle, and crushed under the immense weight of rock above. This process eventually turned the long-dead creatures into fuel.

Offshore oil rigs are built to extract and store oil from the seabed.

MINING FOR FUEL

Mining companies drill through the ocean rock to reach the oil or gas underneath and bring it to the surface. Here, it is refined (meaning purified) to provide fuel for our everyday lives. Oil provides the petroleum and diesel that powers our transportation systems and industry. Gas is used for heating and cooking in our homes. These fuels are also burned in power plants to generate electricity but release harmful pollution as a result (see pages 150–151).

FOSSIL FUEL

Oil and gas under the sea (as well as coal formed on land) are called fossil fuels because of the way they were formed. As dead creatures were broken down between layers of rock and sediment, their bodies produced hydrocarbons (a mixture of hydrogen and carbon), which can be used as fuel. Fossils are the physical remains of these bodies, or their traces and impressions left in the rock, but fossils themselves cannot be used as fuel!

1. The remains of dead plants and animals fall to the ocean floor.

300–400 MILLION YEARS AGO

2. Heat and pressure turn the layers of sediment and organic matter into rock.

50–100 MILLION YEARS AGO

MINING FOR ROCKS

Vast supplies of precious metals and other resources – even diamonds – can also be harvested from the seafloor using mining machines. Copper and nickel are used to make electronics and cables, and cobalt is used to make high-tech devices like smartphones. New technology, including robotically operated vehicles (ROVs), is making deep-sea mining easier, but these activities threaten to destroy precious ocean habitats and are controversial.

Minerals like cobalt are sucked up from the seabed using deep-sea mining machines.

MINING FOR BRINE

Seawater has long been used as a source of salt – including the kind of salt that we eat. Traditionally, sea salt is collected by allowing pools of seawater to evaporate, leaving the salt behind as solid crystals. Sea salt is mostly made of sodium chloride (see page 32), but can also contain other elements, such as potassium, which is extracted and used to make products like fertilizer.

Salt crystals are washed and dried, before being packaged and sold as salt to eat.

SIHWA LAKE
SOUTH KOREA

In 2012, South Korea opened the largest tidal power station anywhere in the world. It uses the energy from tidal water flowing into a giant lake called Sihwa Lake. As the tidal water rushes into the lake, it drives the turbines. These then generate electricity that is used to power the country.

NONRENEWABLE RESOURCES

The riches of the ocean will not last forever. Fossil fuels form very slowly over millions of years, but once they are extracted, they can only be used once – so they are being used up far quicker than they are made. This makes oil and gas "nonrenewable" because they will eventually run out. Drilling for fossil fuels is also destructive: ocean floor habitats are disturbed and sometimes oil leaks out, contaminating the ocean water.

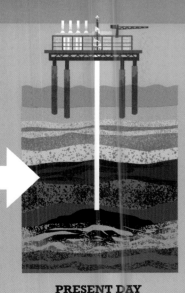

3. The remains of plants and animals (organic matter) produce oil and gas trapped inside the rock.

PRESENT DAY

TIDAL POWER

Some sources of energy are limitless because they are renewable – they will never run out. Modern technology allows us to generate energy from the wind and Sun. In the oceans, the rush of tidal water can be used to generate energy; as moving water flows, it is used to turn generators, which produce power as a result. On the downside, the high costs and environmental impact of building tidal power stations are currently seen as off-putting.

The Rance Tidal Power Station in France was the first in the world.

OCEAN TRAVEL

Before airplanes were invented, all long-distance travel happened via the sea. To this day, ship transportation is an important way of trading goods between countries – many of our clothes and food products arrive from overseas. Ocean voyages are also a popular vacation choice for millions of people worldwide.

HISTORIC PORTS

In ancient history, as people relied more on getting from place to place overseas, coastal ports were built. These had long stone or wood structures called quays, where boats were tied up so that the cargo and passengers could return to land. Some of the biggest ports at the time were established more than 2,000 years ago along the coastlines of the Mediterranean, India, and China, which were important trading routes. Many of these have now worn away due to coastal erosion and crumbled into the sea.

Thirteen Factories was an important region for trade along the Pearl River, China.

Cruise ships enter the Atlantic Ocean from Port Miami.

MODERN PORTS

Today, coastal ports are well connected to places inland via roads, railways, or airports to help make transportation networks more efficient. Some ports are mainly places for cargo and passenger ships, while others are used for fishing or for the navy – a nation's army that operates at sea. Many allow people to enter or leave the country, so passports have to be checked. Port Miami in Florida is the busiest port for vacationers in the world – 1,185 cruise ships passed through here in 2017.

PASSENGER SHIPS

Ferries are used to carry passengers over short distances lasting no more than a day or two. Longer distances are made by cruise ships, which cater for everything a vacationer might need, from restaurants and shops to pools and movie theaters. Some cruise ships carry over 3,000 passengers and are fitted with amusement parks, zip lines, bumper cars, and climbing walls!

Cruises usually last between a week and a month, but a world tour will last around four months!

TRADE BY SEA

Some transported goods (called cargo) are carried by airplane, but this is expensive and very bad for the environment, as planes produce huge amounts of carbon dioxide. As a result, 90 percent of the world's trade is carried by ship across vast distances between international ports – everything from food and cars to fuel and clothes. At any one time, there are about 20 million container ships on the world's oceans.

Huge container ships can carry the equivalent of 745 million bananas!

Tourists watch an orca from a boat.

OCEANS AND TOURISM

Many people like to visit the ocean when they go on vacation. Seaside resorts are popular – especially tropical beaches that stay warm enough to be enjoyed year-round. Ocean wildlife is all part of the attraction, and ecotourism tries to bring tourists closer to wildlife without disturbing the animals. Some travel companies even incorporate whale-watching into holidays!

PORT OF SHANGHAI
CHINA

China's Port of Shanghai is currently the world's biggest container port (where goods are moved from a ship to another mode of transportation, such as a truck). It is the size of 470 soccer fields and the total quay length is 12.4 mi. (20 km)! As well as catering to ships arriving from all over the world, it is an important gateway into China's Yangtze River – the longest river in Asia.

CHINA

JAPAN

SHANGHAI

PHILIPPINES

WATER SPORTS

The oceans offer a perfect environment for a whole host of sports and pastimes. These include activities that harness the power of the wind, such as sailing and windsurfing, others that need the power of an engine, such as jet-skiing and waterskiing, and some that use the force of the ocean itself, riding towering waves using nothing but a surfboard.

SURFING

The first surfers are thought to have lived hundreds of years ago on the islands of the Pacific Ocean, but today people surf all over the world. Good surfing waves depend on how strong the wind is and how far it has traveled across the ocean, called fetch (see pages 46–47). To catch a wave, a surfer needs to paddle fast to get ahead of it as it breaks. Then, once "riding the wave," the aim is to stand up and balance! Advanced surfers can perform tricks, including jumps, called "catching air."

The biggest wave known to have been surfed was an enormous 60 ft. (24 m) tall!

Sailing has been an Olympic sport since 1896.

SAILING

Sailing goes back thousands of years and has enabled ancient civilizations to trade and travel across open water. Sailing boats are powered by the wind, which blows into raised sails and pushes the vessel along. Historically, sails were made of heavy, natural fibers like cotton, but today they are usually manufactured from man-made materials that are tougher, less likely to rot, and are easier to handle. The stronger the wind, the faster a sailing boat will speed along.

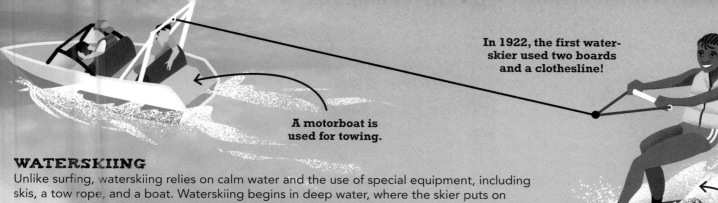

In 1922, the first water-skier used two boards and a clothesline!

A motorboat is used for towing.

The aim is to stay above the water!

WATERSKIING

Unlike surfing, waterskiing relies on calm water and the use of special equipment, including skis, a tow rope, and a boat. Waterskiing begins in deep water, where the skier puts on one or two skis and is attached to the boat. As the boat moves, the skier uses their body strength to pull themselves into an upright position, so they can glide along the water's surface. Waterskiing also needs a "spotter," whose job it is to shout when the skier falls off!

Championships take place around the world, testing speed, agility, and stamina.

JET-SKIING

For those looking for the thrill of riding on the ocean surface at speeds of 65 mph (105 kph), jet-skiing may be just the thing. This small, jet-powered watercraft is usually designed for one to three people – a bit like a motorbike on water. There are three ways to ride: ski style (standing up), runabout (sitting down), or sport (using a smaller, faster model). Advanced jet-skiers can also compete in these styles.

The word "kayak" means "hunter's boat."

KAYAKING

Kayaking can be fast and adrenaline-inducing or a peaceful ride with a view – depending on where you do it. Kayaks sit low in the water, like canoes, but use a paddle with two blades rather than one. Thousands of years ago, the first kayaks were made of driftwood by the Inuit people in the Arctic regions and used for hunting and fishing. Today, sea kayaking is a popular activity all over the world, allowing people to explore hidden coves, coastal caves, and islands.

The sail is used to change direction.

The thinner the board, the faster you will go.

WINDSURFING

Windsurfing is a thrilling mix of two wind-powered disciplines: surfing and sailing. It takes balance and coordination to skim gracefully across the ocean surface, using just a surfboard-sized board and lightweight sail. With practice, windsurfers can perform maneuvers that would be impossible in a sailing boat. Windsurfers were also the first to take on extreme waves, as they were able to maintain speed with – and catch – the biggest, fastest waves.

OCEAN POLLUTION

The oceans help us in so many ways – we rely on them for food, energy, and minerals, and as a means to travel and trade. And yet, the way we currently use the oceans often leaves them damaged and even poisoned. It's becoming increasingly clear just how badly our activities are polluting ocean waters.

Pollution could be industrial chemicals or sewage that is pumped away from land.

WHAT IS POLLUTION?

Pollution happens when human activities contaminate the natural environment – making it dirty or toxic. Pollutants are the nasty substances that cause the damage. Many pollutants, such as carbon dioxide gas or acidic fumes, are unwanted products produced by factories and disposed of as waste. Others, such as plastics or oil, are either deliberately discarded as trash or accidentally spilled.

POLLUTION FROM THE LAND

Fertilizers are chemicals used on fields to improve the growth of crops, but in coastal areas and in estuaries, these can drain into the sea. Here, the nutrients designed for crops can cause an overgrowth of algae, some of which contain chemicals that poison ocean animals if eaten. In some parts of the world, sewage from bathrooms flows into the sea without being treated first. This waste is full of harmful bacteria that can make people and animals very ill.

An overgrowth of algae can change the color of the water and poison ocean life.

OIL SPILLS

Oil is transported around the world in huge tanker ships, but occasionally accidents happen that result in fuel spilling into the ocean – sometimes thousands of tons of it. Oil spills are always damaging to the environment because oil floats on the surface and takes a very long time to disperse. Birds and turtles that live on the water surface can then get coated in oil, which is very difficult to clean up. When oil coats feathers, they lose their waterproofing and no longer keep birds warm, causing them to chill and die. Spilled oil eventually disperses, but can linger for years afterward, often washing ashore and harming the wildlife there, too.

POISONS FROM INDUSTRY

As well as mining on the seafloor, manufacturing products in factories can produce poisonous waste substances, such as lead and mercury. These can end up in the oceans and are consumed by plankton. Plankton are eaten by bigger fish and the poisons build up inside their bodies as it cannot be released. Eventually, top predators like sharks will have eaten so much poison from their prey that it will kill them.

Big fish like sharks eat polluted smaller fish and get poisoned.

Mining accidents cause huge amounts of pollution.

POLLUTION FROM UNDERSEA MINING

When rock on the ocean bed is drilled into for fossil fuel or minerals (see page 144), it can destroy ocean floor habitats and the creatures that live there, as well as kick up a large amount of sediment into the water. This sediment can harm filter-feeding animals as they accidentally consume the tiny bits of rock, which clog their filters and make them less able to catch real food.

Oil is very difficult to clean off and causes severe harm and death to coastal birds.

GREENHOUSE GASES

Some of the biggest threats to the ocean come from polluting gases – especially carbon dioxide produced by burning fossil fuels. Carbon dioxide is called a greenhouse gas because it traps heat inside the Earth's atmosphere and so increases global temperatures – similar to how a garden greenhouse traps the Sun's warmth inside. Carbon dioxide also makes ocean waters more acidic, which is particularly damaging for creatures with delicate shells or skeletons (see page 153).

CARBON DIOXIDE

Our modern lives, with the rise of industry and intensive farming, are releasing more polluting gases into the air than ever before. Many of these gases, such as carbon dioxide, are causing damaging long-term changes to the oceans of the world.

THE GREENHOUSE EFFECT

Most of the air we breathe is made up of nitrogen and oxygen. Only a tiny fraction – just 0.04 percent – is carbon dioxide. But this tiny amount is enough to form a heat-trapping layer in the atmosphere and stop the oceans from freezing solid. As the Sun's rays warm the Earth's surface, some of this energy is absorbed and the rest is reflected away from our planet. With higher levels of carbon dioxide in the atmosphere, more of the Sun's energy gets trapped there, making the environment warmer. We call this global warming.

SUN

SPACE

Some of the heat escapes into space.

CLOUD

ATMOSPHERE

The Sun's rays warm the Earth.

Some of the heat trapped by greenhouse gases travels back to Earth.

EARTH

RISING GREENHOUSE GASES

Without greenhouse gases, the Earth would be a snowball planet (see page 23), but over the last 200 years, our global industries have pumped huge amounts of carbon dioxide into the atmosphere – and levels are now too high. An extra greenhouse gas, methane, is produced by farmed cattle (a result of our demand for meat) that burp or fart it out. All this has increased average global temperatures by around one degree, which doesn't sound like a lot, but it is far warmer than is natural and has had a huge impact on habitats worldwide.

EFFECTS ON THE POLAR SEAS

With more greenhouse gases trapped in the atmosphere, ocean temperatures are rising, too. The most obvious effect of global warming can be seen in the poles – where the ice caps are rapidly melting and getting smaller. As ice melts into water, it flows into the oceans and sea levels rise. Less ice also means less sunshine is reflected away from the Earth (the albedo effect, see page 120) – which increases the temperatures in polar regions even further.

Fish such as whale sharks rely on the circulation of ocean currents to provide them with food.

SEA LEVELS AND OCEAN CURRENTS

Rising sea levels caused by melting polar ice makes flooding in coastal areas more likely and could force many people to leave their homes. Our melting ice caps are also likely to have a big impact on global ocean currents (see pages 44–45), as more and more cold glacial water enters the world's oceans. The flow of currents is likely to slow down, which will affect the supply of nutrients circling around the world and reduce the numbers of plankton – an essential part of ocean food chains.

OCEAN ACIDITY

As well as being a greenhouse gas, carbon dioxide makes water more acidic. When carbon dioxide is absorbed by the ocean, it reacts with the seawater to form carbonic acid – so more carbon dioxide means more acid. This damages the hard, chalky shells of many marine animals, particularly those of tiny planktonic creatures, causing their shells to dissolve.

Acid eats away at the shells of invertebrates.

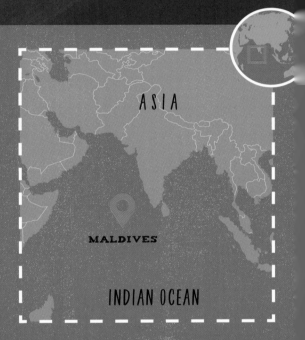

ASIA

MALDIVES

INDIAN OCEAN

MALDIVES
INDIAN OCEAN

The Maldives is an island nation located in the north Indian Ocean. The region is made entirely of low-lying coral rock. This means that if sea levels continue to rise as they currently are, the Maldives will be completely underwater by the year 2100. And it's not just islands that are under threat. It is predicted that around 300 million homes around the world will flood at least once a year by 2050 unless carbon dioxide levels are drastically reduced.

If all the Antarctic ice melted, sea levels would rise 197 ft. (60 m), flooding coastal towns and cities.

PLASTIC IN THE OCEAN

Much of the world's discarded trash ends up in the oceans, and a whopping 80 percent of it is plastic. Huge amounts of plastic pollute the oceans and shorelines, and part of the problem is how difficult it is to get rid of. The best way to reduce the harm that plastic is causing is to say no to single-use plastics, such as straws, and recycle or reuse any plastic that is unavoidable.

THE PROBLEM WITH PLASTIC

Most plastic takes hundreds or even thousands of years to break down – nearly every piece of plastic ever made is thought to still exist in some way. Plastic cannot be well disposed of by burning (like other types of trash), because this releases poisonous gases. And rather than decomposing naturally like organic materials (think of how food waste slowly mulches down), plastic breaks down into smaller and smaller pieces that then pose a threat to ocean life.

Around 50 percent of plastic is used just once, then thrown away.

PLASTIC IN THE OCEANS

When plastic is washed into the ocean, it is frequently mistaken for food by ocean animals such as birds and whales. When it is swallowed, plastic leads to blockages in animals' guts, which eventually kills them. Even in seawater, plastic takes a very long time to break down – it stays as tiny fragments, called microplastic, that get eaten by plankton and find their way into food chains.

MICROPLASTICS

Any plastic that is less than 0.2 in. (5 mm) long, smaller than a grain of rice, is called a microplastic. These are found nearly everywhere – even in the very deepest parts of the ocean and inside the stomachs of birds and whales. Small plastic pellets, called nurdles, are made during the plastic production process and then enter our oceans. Other types of man-made microplastics are added to body washes as "microbeads." When washed away, these end up in lakes and oceans worldwide.

Microplastics are now found in nearly all waters worldwide, from the open oceans to rivers inland.

GHOST FISHING

Plastic has been mass produced since its invention because it has such a wide range of uses – even fishing nets can be made from plastic. These nets are cheap and long-lasting, but when they are lost or abandoned at sea, plastic nets pose a threat to ocean wildlife. They take many years (sometimes hundreds!) to break down, and during this time, ocean animals, including whales and dolphins, can continue to get trapped in them. This is called ghost fishing.

CLEANING UP THE OCEAN

Plastic floating in the ocean gathers in places where there are circular water currents called gyres (see page 45). There are five ocean garbage patches in the world and over 5 trillion pieces of plastic floating around in the open ocean. The biggest, the Great Pacific Garbage Patch, is about three times the size of France. Organizations are trying to clean up these ocean "trash sites" by using lines of floating trash collectors that capture and keep hold of plastic debris.

A giant floating garbage collector was towed into the Pacific Ocean in 2018.

REDUCING PLASTIC

One way to reduce the amount of plastic that enters the environment is by recycling it – but many of our recycling methods still need to be improved. Another is to replace plastic products, such as disposable cutlery and plastic bags, with materials that are biodegradable, like bamboo and cotton – which can break down naturally in the environment.

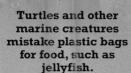

Turtles and other marine creatures mistake plastic bags for food, such as jellyfish.

Reusable water bottle

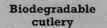

Biodegradable cutlery

HENDERSON ISLAND
SOUTH PACIFIC OCEAN

Henderson Island in the South Pacific is one of the most remote spots of land anywhere on the planet. It is uninhabited (no humans live there permanently) and was long thought to be one of the few places on Earth largely unharmed by humans. But a study in 2017 revealed that despite its isolation, it is packed with plastic trash! More than 18 tons of plastic have washed up on its shores, showing how far-reaching and long-lasting the effects of plastic waste are.

PACIFIC OCEAN

HENDERSON ISLAND

UNDER THREAT

Human activities around the world are threatening many ocean habitats. Some of these habitats, such as coral reefs, are home to so many different kinds of life that if these habitats disappear, large numbers of species will suddenly become extinct. Imagine our vibrant tropical reefs turning white and lifeless, or the Arctic homes of the polar bears melting into the sea – these are the environmental challenges currently facing our planet.

THREATS TO THE COASTLINE

There is a wide range of different habitats around coastlines – from rocky shores and sandy beaches to salt marshes, mudflats, and mangrove swamps. These coastlines are popular places for people to live and vacation, and new homes and vacation resorts are built here. As a result, unique and precious habitats are sometimes destroyed to make way for man-made structures.

THREATS TO THE OPEN OCEAN

Out at sea, pollution from oceangoing ships and mining for minerals has destroyed many habitats, leaving species with nowhere to live, while industrial fishing and whaling practices have driven many species to the brink of extinction (see pages 142–143).

Tourism can help local people earn money but also poses big threats to the environment.

GREAT BARRIER REEF
AUSTRALIA

GREAT BARRIER REEF

AUSTRALIA

PACIFIC OCEAN

Australia's Great Barrier Reef is the largest coral reef on Earth, covering an area of 132,973 sq. mi. (344,400 sq km). But even here, the rate of coral growth has dropped by 50 percent since 1985 – and rising ocean temperatures are causing widespread coral bleaching. Even though these habitats have existed for millions of years, there's a chance that children born today may never witness a thriving coral reef. Long stretches of the reef have already died, reflecting the extreme effects of global warming on ocean wildlife.

KEMP'S RIDLEY SEA TURTLE

Over the years, hunting, being trapped in fishing nets, and the loss of nesting beaches to pollution and human developments have seen the Kemp's ridley sea turtle pushed to the edge of extinction. These turtles are not alone; out of the seven sea turtle species around the world, six are classified as threatened or endangered by human actions.

Kemp's ridley sea turtles are extremely rare.

Baby sharks are fished by mistake.

THE CASE OF THE COMMON SKATE

As the name suggests, the common skate was once very common – in fact, it was one of the most abundant fish species in the North Atlantic and a popular catch for fishermen. But overfishing has driven it almost to the point of extinction. It is now missing from around most European coastlines. Numbers are still decreasing, and it is ranked as critically endangered.

A common skate can grow almost 10 ft. (3 m) in length!

BYCATCH

Fishing, especially with big nets, is not a selective way of fishing. Nets catch all kinds of creatures, some of which can be sold as food and others that are unwanted. These unwanted animals are called bycatch and include a huge number of seabirds, dolphins, and turtles. The trapped, and often injured, bycatch animals are discarded dead or dying – this is a huge conservation issue for many species around the world.

THE CASE OF THE BLUE WHALE

Blue whales – the largest species of animal ever to have lived – came close to extinction because of overhunting. Tens of thousands were killed when whaling peaked 100 years ago. Blue whales live a long time but have a slow breeding rate, which puts them more at risk. Numbers have been increasing since whaling was banned – there are an estimated 5,000 to 15,000 today – but they are still ranked as endangered,

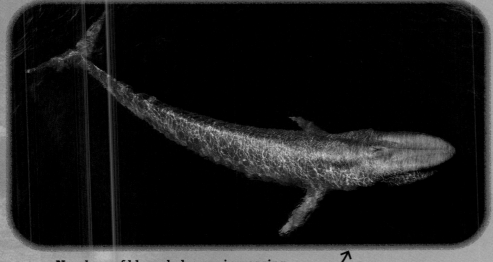

Numbers of blue whales are increasing, but lots more needs to be done.

THE CASE OF THE SCALLOPED HAMMERHEAD

Some fishing practices are especially damaging, wasteful, and cruel to the animals. Shark fins are prized for their delicious flavor in some countries and are eaten as a treat. But this comes at a horrible cost to the sharks: they are caught, their fins removed, and the living animals returned to the sea, where they will eventually die from starvation because they cannot swim without their fins. Scalloped hammerheads, now an endangered species, are especially targeted because of their large fins.

Shark fin soup was traditionally served as a celebratory dish.

CONSERVATION IN ACTION

All around the world, people are taking steps to help protect the oceans and their wildlife, helping to ensure that future generations can enjoy them, too. From specially trained scientists who work in the ocean, to groups of people who come together to help clean up polluted beaches – there are all kinds of ways that people (including you!) can help.

A whale shark tagged with a radio device.

CONSERVATION SCIENTISTS

The more we know about the oceans and ocean wildlife, the better chance we have of protecting them from harm. Many scientists are specialists on a particular species and use technology to help study their behavior further. Sometimes, animals that migrate are tagged with a radio device that sends out signals that can be tracked, so that their routes can be mapped out and protected.

Protestors campaigning against whaling

CAMPAIGNERS

When the true extent of whaling – and the harm it was causing to whale populations – became known, many people campaigned to have whaling stopped. While scientists provided evidence for the threat of extinction, public pressure on governments helped push the message further. In 1986, commercial whaling was banned (see page 143).

WILDLIFE WARDENS

In many protected habitats around the world, wildlife wardens are employed to help ensure that marine animals stay safe from harm, such as by controlling fishing or protecting the nesting sites of birds or turtles. These wardens might also visit schools to talk about the importance of ocean conservation with children, who may also want to help save ocean wildlife.

Collecting trash is a great way to help protect our coastlines.

Boat tours allow people to learn more about ocean wildlife from guides.

OCEAN GUIDES

Experienced divers and biologists can help tourists see ocean wildlife, and watch their natural behavior, by acting as guides. Whether they help people spot whales, or help them identify animals on a coral reef during a scuba dive, this kind of ecotourism enables people to experience how spectacular and valuable the oceans are.

ATLANTIC OCEAN

UK

EUROPE

UNITED KINGDOM
... AND WORLDWIDE

Cleanup events are a fun and effective way to protect our oceans. Organizations like Plastic Patrol, set up in the UK in 2016, arrange cleanup events that bring communities together to save their local waterways. The first cleanups were in the UK, but they were so popular that events now run in Europe and the US.

BEACH CLEANUPS

More than 30 years ago, a group of American volunteers started an organization called International Coastal Cleanup. Now represented in 100 countries around the world, this huge network of volunteers clears up the trash found along coastlines. Organizations like this exist all over the world, many of which are set up by young people who want to ensure a healthy planet for their generation (and future generations). Together, volunteer groups get people directly involved in the conservation of the ocean and have a noticeable impact on local ocean habitats.

GLOSSARY

AMPHIBIOUS Adapted to living both on land and in water.

ARCHAEOLOGIST A person who studies the history of humankind by finding and analysing artifacts and remains.

ASTEROID A rocky object that orbits the Sun.

ATMOSPHERE The layer of gases surrounding our planet.

BIODIVERSITY A measure of the number of different species of living things in a habitat.

BUOYANT When something is light enough to float on top of a liquid or gas.

CELLS The smallest units that make up a living thing, also known as the building blocks of life.

CLIMATE The usual weather conditions found in a particular region, measured over a long time period.

COLONIZE The process of a species spreading to a new area and establishing a group called a colony.

COMPASS A device used for finding direction with a needle that points north.

CONDENSE When a vapor or gas turns into a liquid; for example, when water vapor in the air condenses to form clouds.

CONSERVATION The preservation and protection of plant and animal species, natural habitats, or areas of special interest.

CONTAMINATE To make something less pure by mixing it with something unclean or poisonous.

CONTINENTAL CRUST The thick pieces of Earth's crust that make up large landmasses called continents.

CORAL BLEACHING When living coral expels the colorful algae living inside it and turns white as a result.

DILUTE To make a liquid weaker (less concentrated) by adding water or another liquid.

DIVERSITY see "biodiversity."

DNA Short for "deoxyribonucleic acid." DNA is stored inside the cells of living things and carries information about how a living thing will look and function.

ECOTOURISM Vacations involving visiting natural places and seeing wildlife, done in a way that helps to protect the environment.

ELEMENT The building blocks that make up all matter. A pure element is made up of just one type of atom.

ENDANGERED A species that is endangered is at risk of becoming extinct and disappearing forever, often due to loss of habitat or climate change.

EQUATOR An imaginary line that runs around the middle of Earth, dividing the planet into the northern and southern hemispheres.

EVOLUTION The way in which populations of living things change over many generations, resulting in new species.

EXTINCTION The disappearance of a particular species when no living examples of that species are left in the world.

FOSSILS The preserved remains, or traces, of ancient plants or animals.

GEOLOGISTS Scientists who study the history and physical features of Earth, particularly its rocks.

GLAND A part of the body that releases substances that perform specific jobs inside the body.

GRAVITATIONAL PULL The attraction (or pull) between two objects with mass, caused by the force of gravity.

HABITAT The environment in which a plant or animal makes its home.

HEMISPHERE Half of a sphere. Earth is divided into the northern hemisphere and southern hemisphere by the equator.

HERBIVORE An animal that gets its energy from eating only plants.

ICE AGE A period when Earth's global temperatures drop significantly, and polar ice caps expand to cover huge areas of land.

INCUBATE When an animal sits on its eggs to keep them warm, allowing the baby inside to develop and eventually hatch.

LARVAE The youngest form of an animal after hatching, before maturing into its adult form.

METAMORPHOSIS The dramatic transformation that some living things go through before reaching their adult form.

MICROBES Microscopic organisms that are all around us but are too small to see with the naked eye. They include bacteria, viruses, algae, and fungi.

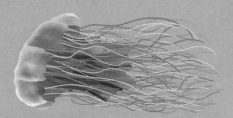
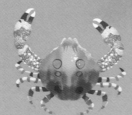

MOLECULE A tiny particle of a substance. For instance, a molecule of water is the smallest amount of water that can exist.

MOLTEN An object or material that is so hot it has changed into liquid form.

NERVES Inside the body, nerves carry electrical messages to and from the brain. Nerves make up the nervous system, which controls many of the body's functions.

NUTRIENTS Substances in food that all living things need to survive, function, and grow.

ORGANISMS Includes all living things, from elephants to seaweed.

PHILOSOPHER A person who studies ideas about the world, people, and the meaning of life with the aim of gaining greater wisdom.

PHOTOSYNTHESIS A process that happens inside green plants and algae where light energy is used to turn carbon dioxide and water into food for them to survive.

PIGMENT A substance that gives color to another material.

PLANKTON Living things that float in water, including microscopic plants (phytoplankton) and animals (zooplankton).

POLAR Relating to the regions surrounding Earth's North and South Poles.

PRECIPITATION Water particles that fall from clouds and reach the ground as either rain, snow, sleet, or hail, depending on the weather conditions.

PREDATOR An animal that hunts and kills other animals for food.

PREHISTORIC The period of time before recorded history.

RECYCLED The process by which materials and objects are reused or repurposed instead of being thrown away.

REGENERATION The process by which plants and animals can replace damaged or lost body parts, such as regrowing lost limbs.

REPRODUCE The biological process whereby an organism produces offspring (young).

RESPIRATION A chemical reaction that happens inside all living cells to release energy for survival.

SATELLITE A natural or artificial object that is in orbit around a larger object in space; for example, a moon is a natural satellite of a planet.

SCAVENGER An animal that seeks out and feeds on scraps of discarded food or decaying material.

SEDIMENT Particles of material, such as sand or stones, that are carried by water and eventually deposited (dropped).

SOLAR ECLIPSE When the Moon passes in front of the Sun and casts a shadow on parts of Earth's surface.

SPAWN When a female fish or other aquatic animal releases many unfertilized eggs into the water, some of which may be fertilized by a male of the same species.

STONE AGE A prehistoric period when people made simple tools and weapons out of natural materials such as stone, wood, and bone.

SUPERCONTINENT A giant landmass made up of two or more of Earth's continents. Supercontinents are formed and destroyed as continents drift over time.

SUPEROCEAN A giant ocean that surrounds a supercontinent.

SURFACE AREA A measurement of the amount of space taken up by a surface.

SUSTAINABLE A way of doing something that is not harmful to the environment and doesn't use up limited natural resources.

TEMPERATE Relating to the mild weather experienced in Earth's temperate regions, which exist between the hot tropics (near the equator) and the icy poles.

TOXIC A substance that is harmful or poisonous to living things or the environment.

TURBINE A mechanical device made of a central shaft with blades attached. The turbine rotates when air, steam, or water passes through it and generates power, such as electricity.

VAPOR A substance that is suspended (floating) in air.

WARM-BLOODED Relating to animals that can maintain a stable body temperature and generate their own heat, even when their surroundings are cold.

WAVELENGTH The length between crests (highest points) of a wave. The wavelength of light energy affects the color of the light that is detected.

INDEX

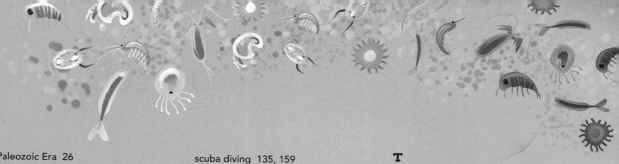

PICTURE CREDITS

Front Cover (tl): NASA; (bc) Shutterstock / z576; (cr) Shutterstock / Andrea Izzotti

Alamy: p24 (cl) Xinhua p26 (cl) Stocktrek Images p52 (cl) Science & Science p69 (t) Paulo Oliveira. **Dreamstime:** p128 (b) Steven Huff. **Ella Sophonisba Hergesheimer** p130 (t). **Getty Images:** p18 (bl) Stocktrek Images p27 (b) Nobumichi / Stocktrek Images p30 (b) estt p38 (b) Universal History Archive p54–55 548901005677 p55 (tl) apomares p59 (c) Cultura RF / Alexander Semenov p61 (t) Didier BRANDELET / Contributor p62 (bl) rusm p66 (tl) PhotoPlus Magazine / Contributor (bc) Gerard Soury p67 (c) tunart p69 (tr) Richard Robinson p70 (t) Hoberman Collection / Contributor p73 (tl) skynesher (cr) Beth Swanson (bl) Henner Damke (br) bearacreative p77 (bl) Marvin del Cid p111 (t) (r) Ralph White (cl) (b) Universal History Archive / Contributor p126 (t) Wolfgang Kaehler / Contributor p128 (l) Zhang Peng / Contributor p131 (tl) Fritz Goro / Contributor p132 (l) ROMEO GACAD / Staff p134 (t) Jeff Rotman p135 (c) Loic Lagarde / Contributor (b) BORIS HORVAT / Staff p138 (l) Olivia Harris / Stringer (b)

Epics / Contributor p139 (t) Patrick Durand / Contributor (c) NRK/POOL / Contributor p141 (tl) DEA PICTURE LIBRARY / Contributor p143 (bl) Jeff Rotman p143 (br) ZU_09 p151 (t) Handout / Handout p155 (r) MediaNews Group / East Bay Times p157 (c) Paul Kay p158 (l) Gerard Soury (b) Hulton Deutsch / Contributor p149 (t) Education Images / Contributor. **Glenn Singleman** p137 (c). **NASA:** p39 (t) Jacques Descloitres, MODIS Rapid Response Team, NASA / GSFC p114 (t) Jacques Descloitres, MODIS Rapid Response Team, NASA / GSFC p115 (bl)) Jacques Descloitres, MODIS Rapid Response Team, NASA / GSFC NASA p131 (c) Ball Aerospace / NASA. **Nature Picture Library** p141 (t) Michael Pitts. **NOAA National Ocean Service:** p43 (b) NOAA p70 (b) NOAA Okeanos Explorer Program, INDEX-SATAL 2010, NOAA / OER p107 (b) NOAA Office of Ocean Exploration and Research, Gulf of Mexico 2017 p108 (l) NOAA p109 (t) NOAA p122 (l) NOAA p130 (l) NOAA p135 (b) NOAA / Schmidt Ocean Institute p136 (b) NOAA / Robert Carmichael / Project Baseline. **Ortelius** p14 (b). **Racklever** p129 (bl). **Science Photo** p26 (bc) Richard Bizley. **Shutterstock:** p1 Leonardo Gonzalez p6 (c) Dima Zel (t) divedog (l) Divelvanov p7 (t) JIALING CAI (r) Anton Watman (b) Tory Kallman p8 (l) Adwo (b) Zabotnova Inna p9 (t) Lefteris Papaulakis p10 (cl) elladoro p11 (tr) MikeDrago.cz p12 (l) szefei p13 (t) byvalet (b) AJP p15 (b) Mazur Travel p16 (l) Alexey Suloev p17 (t) polarman p18 (tl) Vladi333 p21 (tl) VicPhotoria p22 (bl) CHIARI VFX p23 (t) Benny Marty (br) Discovod p24 (bl) Dotted Yeti p26 (bl) Warpaint p28–29 (c) Daniel Eskridge p29 (cr) SciePro p31 (tl) Willyam Bradberry (tr) kajornyot wildlife photography p32–33 MstudioG p33 (t) murattellioglu p33 (r) Rich Carey (c) Rattiya Thongdumhyu p34 (bl) Henri Vandelanotte (br) Shaiith p35 (tr) MagicPitzy (c) Graffitimi p36 (t) KrimKate (bl) alex7370 p37 (cr) Fata Morgana by Andrew Marriott (br) weicool p39 (r) Damsea p45 (t) Rainer Lesniewski p47 (r) Pawel Kazmierczak (b) Fly_

and_Dive p49 (tl) Tom Clausen (tr) Vintagepix (cr) Richard P Long p52 c Elif Bayraktar p53 (t) Rattiya Thongdumhyu (cr) Ralf Liebhold p54 (b) ChWeiss (cl) Daniel Poloha (cr) J Need p55 (tl) Peter Wollinga p56 (t) LanKS p58 (tl) Barelli Paolo p59 (r) Peter Leahy (bc) HotFlash (br) David Havel p60 (t) ScubaPonnie p62 (br) Dan Bagur p63 (tl) Suwat Sirivucharungchit p63 (tr) xbrchx p64–65 Lerner Vadim p64 (t) Apple Pho (cl) JetKat p65 (tr) worldclassphoto (br) Joe Belanger p66 (c) Andrey Nosik (bl) Vojce p67 (t) DeeAnn Cranston (br) zaferkizilkaya p68 (l) Sergey Uryadnikov (c) Martin Prochazkacz (bl) Ken Kiefer p69 (b) Dirk van der Heide p70–71 Leonardo Gonzalez p70 (c) Vladimir Wrangel p71 (t) AdrianNunez p72 Dwi Agung Sulistyo p72 (l) ADRIAN DIAZ CADAVID p74 (c) Piotr Pawlikiewicz (bl) Alizada Studios p75 (tr) Dannis Jacobsen (c) Jean-Edouard Rozey p76–77 FamVeld p76 (bc) David Evison (br) Kalaeva p77 (tl) Krzysztof Bargiel (tr) SergeUWPhoto p78 (t) Tory Kallman (l) wildestanimal p80 (l) Shelly Mack (br) TravelMediaProductions p82 (tl) Martin M303 p83 (tl) Tricobliss (r) WASANA WONGPURANANONT (b) David Holmes Geography p84 (t) Alexlky p85 (t) Alexander Varbenov (r) Icruci (l) yxowert (b) Heather Lucia Snow p86–87 Brady Barrineau p86 (t) BGSmith (l) LABETAA Andre p87 (t) Vladimir Wrangel (bl) Heidi Killick p88–89 David Min p88 (l) Jeff Holcombe p89 (t) HurleySB (tr) Simon Dannhauer (tr) Rich Carey (cr) Sergey Fatin (bl) Vinicius Moreira da Silva (br) Paruj Akranurakkul p90 (cl) Otto Born p91 (bl) tartmany p92–93 Animaflora PicsStock p93 (t) jopelka (c) Ethan Daniels (r) Lertwit Sasipreyajun p94 (l) aquapix (b) Richard Whitcombe p95 (t) Ethan Daniels (b) Fotos593 p96 (t) blue-sea.cz p97 (tr) superjoseph (l) Copyright (cr) Fabio Lamanna p98–99 Ethan Daniels p98 (l) Dan Bagur (b) Keneva Photography p99 (t) Ethan Daniels (c) Laura Dinraths p100 (l) Niar p102 (l) Robert mcgillivray p103 (tr) Johnny Adolphson p106 (l) NatureDiver p109 (b) Greg

Amptman p114–115 Fabio Lamanna p114 (bl) Brian Lasenby p115 (tr) tito0nz p116–117 Joe West p116 (l) Robert Crow p116 (b) wildestanimal p117 (r) Ricardo_Dias p118–119 R McIntyre p118 (l) Ethan Daniels p119 (c) Ethan Daniels (t) Everett Historical p120–121 Tyler Olson p120 (cr) JoannaPerchaluk p121 (c) Ondrej Prosicky p123 (tr) Robert mcgillivray p124 (b) Keith Michael Taylor p125 (t) Nikolai Denisov (bl) SZakharov p126 (b) Alexey Seafarer p127 (t) Menno Schaefer p129 (c) Eileen Tweedy p129 (cr) Andrey Armyagov p131 (b) sdecoret p133 (bl) RugliG (br) Yann Hubert p134 (tr) Vova Shevchuk (br) BlueOrange Studio p134–135 (c) Aniwat phromrungsee p138–139 Sven Hansche p139 (b) Adam Ke p140 (c) Nejdet Duzen p142–143 amnat30 p142 (l) JueWorn p144–155 Red Ivory p145 (r) Bjoern Wylezich (c) Fahroni (b) Francois BOIZOT p146–147 Alex Kolokythas Photography p146 (l) Mia2you (bl) Ruth Peterkin p147 (tr) Tory Kallman p148–149 EpicStockMedia p148 (bl) Theodore Trimmer p149 (t) Lee Bernard (cr) BlueOrange Studio p150–151 Justin Sullivan / Staff p150 (l) Vereshcagin Dmitry (bl) T.W. van Urk p151 (b) VLADJ55 p152 (b) EB Adventure Photography p153 (t) chatchai Kusolsinchai (c) Ethan Daniels (b) Bernhard Staehli p154–155 (t) Willyam Bradberry (b) Eric Dale p154 (l) Rich Carey p155 (tr) Rich Carey (c) Igisheva Maria (cr) Aleksandrs Samuilovs p156 (c) SVongpra p157 (t) Prentiss Findlay (tr) Andreas Altenburger (cl) Chase Dekker p157 (br) Janos Rautonen p158–159 WAYHOME studio p159 (cr) Jekurantodistaja. **Talifero** p26 (tl). **The Hongs at Canton**, circa 1820 / unknown p146 (t). **U.S. Navy** photo by General Dynamics Electric Boat p136 (bl). **United States Naval Observatory** p130 (b) Maury, Matthew Fontaine; Guthrie, John Julien; May, R. L.; United States. Bureau Of Ordnance And Hydrography; United States. Hydrographic Office. **Victor-ny** p10 (b)

Illustrations by Daniel Limon